500   3
           /E

D0441783

The American History Series

SERIES EDITORS

John Hope Franklin, *Duke University*

Abraham S. Eisenstadt, *Brooklyn Colle*

Arthur S. Link
Princeton University
GENERAL EDITOR FOR HISTORY

Ralph B. Levering
DAVIDSON COLLEGE

The Cold War

1945–1987

SECOND EDITION

HARLAN DAVIDSON, INC.
ARLINGTON HEIGHTS, ILLINOIS 60004

Copyright © 1982, 1988
Harlan Davidson, Inc.
All rights reserved

This book, or parts thereof, must not be used or reproduced in any manner without written permission. For information, address the publisher, Harlan Davidson, Inc., 3110 North Arlington Heights Road, Arlington Heights, Illinois 60004-1592.

Library of Congress Cataloging-in-Publication Data

Levering, Ralph B.
    The cold war, 1945–1987 / Ralph B. Levering.
       p. cm. — (The American history series)
    Rev. and updated ed. of: The cold war, 1945–1972. c1982.
    Bibliography: p.
    Includes index.
    ISBN 0-88295-858-5
    1. United States—Foreign relations—1945-   2. World
politics—1945-   3. United States—Foreign relations—Soviet Union.
4. Soviet Union—Foreign relations—United States. I. Levering,
Ralph B. Cold war, 1945–1972. II. Title. III. Series: American
history series (Arlington Heights, Ill.)
E744.L4943   1988
327.73—dc19   87-25459
                                                    CIP

Cover illustration: "The High Flyers of Geneva," by Hermann Degkwitz, originally published on the cover of *Der Spiegel*. Reproduced courtesy of Prof. Hermann Degkwitz.

Manufactured in the United States of America
92 91 90 89 88 LC 2 3 4 5 6

To my sisters and brother
Lois, Betsy, Montague, Merry, Frank—
Examples and friends

FOREWORD

Every generation writes its own history, for the reason that it sees the past in the foreshortened perspective of its own experience. This has certainly been true of the writing of American history. The practical aim of our historiography is to offer us a more certain sense of where we are going by helping us understand the road we took in getting where we are. If the substance and nature of our historical writing is changing, it is precisely because our own generation is redefining its direction, much as the generation that preceded us redefined theirs. We are seeking a newer direction, because we are facing new problems, changing our values and premises, and shaping new institutions to meet new needs. Thus, the vitality of the present inspires the vitality of our writing about our past. Today's scholars are hard at work reconsidering every major field of our history: its politics, diplomacy, economy, society, mores, values, sexuality, and status, ethnic, and race relations. No less significantly, our scholars are using newer modes of investigation to probe the ever-expanding domain of the American past.

Our aim, in this American History Series, is to offer the reader a survey of what scholars are saying about the central themes and issues of American history. To present these themes and issues, we have invited scholars who have made notable contributions to the respective fields in which they are writing.

Each volume offers the reader a sufficient factual and narrative account for perceiving the larger dimensions of its particular subject. Addressing their respective themes, our authors have undertaken, moreover, to present the conclusions derived by the principal writers on these themes. Beyond that, the authors present their own conclusions about those aspects of their respective subjects that have been matters of difference and controversy. In effect, they have written not only about where the subject stands in today's historiography but also about where they stand on their subject. Each volume closes with an extensive critical essay on the writings of the major authorities on its particular theme.

The books in this series are designed for use in both basic and advanced courses in American history. Such a series has a particular utility in times such as these, when the traditional format of our American history courses is being altered to accommodate a greater diversity of texts and reading materials. The series offers a number of distinct advantages. It extends and deepens the dimensions of course work in American history. In proceeding beyond the confines of the traditional textbook, it makes clear that the study of our past is, more than the student might otherwise infer, at once complex, sophisticated, and profound. It presents American history as a subject of continuing vitality and fresh investigation. The work of experts in their respective fields, it opens up to the student the rich findings of historical inquiry. It invites the student to join, in major fields of research, the many groups of scholars who are pondering anew the central themes and problems of our past. It challenges the student to participate actively in exploring American history and to collaborate in the creative and rigorous adventure of seeking out its wider reaches.

John Hope Franklin
Abraham S. Eisenstadt

CONTENTS

PREFACE TO THE
SECOND EDITION

The primary goal of the second edition is to expand the book through the Carter and Reagan years. The harsh words and confrontational deeds of the late 1970s and early 1980s made it clear that the Cold War had not ended a decade earlier, as some political leaders and commentators had hoped during the halcyon days of détente. Recurring patterns in Soviet-American relations were again visible: competition in weaponry, with each nation claiming to be behind and accusing the other of striving for superiority; conflict in the Third World, with each side insisting that it favored local self-determination while the other was seeking domination; and a wide range of ideological and economic competition that poisoned the atmosphere and increased the difficulty of resolving specific issues as they arose. Studying the recent period in Soviet-American relations not only increases one's knowledge of contemporary history; it also can lead, through comparisons and contrasts with earlier periods, to a deeper understanding of the Cold War as a whole.

Chapter 4, covering the years 1973–1987, is entirely new to this edition; the epilogue has been largely rewritten; and the bibliography, while necessarily selective, has been expanded and brought up-to-date. I was tempted to make changes in the earlier chapters as well: to present more information on economic aspects of U.S. and Soviet foreign policy, for example, or to go into detail on U.S. interventions in Latin America and Africa in the 1950s and 1960s. But then I realized that all such changes would increase the book's length beyond what already was occurring through the addition of a new chapter. Thus, in order to keep the book relatively short and accessible to a wide range of students, the earlier chapters remain virtually unchanged. I trust my fellow teachers to give lectures to fill the gaps that they consider most important, and I hope that they will encourage students interested in learning more about particular topics to consult the works cited in the bibliographical essay.

I wish to thank those who have read and criticized either the entire book or specific chapters: Aleine Austin, Robert A. Divine, John Lewis Gaddis, Maureen Hewitt, Wallace Irwin, Jr., Walter LaFeber, Patricia W. Levering, Arthur S. Link, Elizabeth Morgan, Thomas R. Maddux, Louis Ortmeyer, David Patterson, Jack Perry, Harry Stegmaier, Jr., Samuel Walker, Robert Williams, and, of course, the editors of this series. I also am grateful to my students during the past fifteen years at Davidson College, Earlham College, and Western Maryland College. They have helped me to keep learning about the past and caring about our common future.

Yalta and Other
Cold War Myths

At least in the European theater, the end of World War II was in sight by the time President Franklin D. Roosevelt prepared to attend the important meeting of "Big Three" Allied leaders at Yalta from February 4 to 11, 1945. Leaving Washington by battleship shortly after his inauguration on January 20 for an unprecedented fourth term, Roosevelt arrived on the island of Malta in the Mediterranean on February 2. He then proceeded by plane to Yalta, a resort town in southern Russia[1] which still showed clear signs of the devastation inflicted by the invading German armies earlier in the war. Roosevelt was suffering from the serious circulatory problems that sapped his strength during the last year of his life; but according to Charles Bohlen and other American officials who accompanied him to Yalta, the president's illness did not affect significantly his conduct of diplomacy.

Roosevelt was under substantial domestic pressure to obtain at Yalta a commitment to a postwar world based on such high-minded ideals as self-determination for all peoples and trust in a new international organization to keep the peace. More precisely, according to a growing chorus of criticism in the press and in Congress, the president needed to insure that Russia would participate in the war against Japan after Germany was defeated, that it would not try to dominate Poland and other East European nations, and that it would participate enthusiastically in the proposed United Nations.

Roosevelt was well aware by the beginning of 1945 that these and other demands could not be achieved completely and would require compromises, but he limited his public statements in 1944 and early 1945 to optimistic generalities. Although this approach may well have lessened public disillusionment with Allied relations during wartime, it added to the pressure on the president to maintain at least the appearance of unity between the United States, Great Britain, and the Soviet Union.

To Roosevelt's liberal supporters, the possible collapse of the Grand Alliance was a horrid nightmare. If the Big Three did not find a way to maintain amicable relations, victory in the war might well be jeopardized. But even if victory occurred, animosity between the two most powerful nations in history might well lead to a new arms race, to a new system of alliances, and ulti-

---

[1] The terms "Russia" and "Soviet Union" are used in this book as synonyms, both referring to the nation officially called the Union of Soviet Socialist Republics. Similarly, "America" and "United States" refer to the United States of America.

mately to a third and even more devastating world war. It also would debilitate the new United Nations even before it got off the ground. "I am convinced that we can no longer afford the drawing room or editorial room pleasure of asking ourselves, 'Can we get along with Russia?'" journalist Richard Lauterbach wrote in a typical plea for friendship in 1944. "We must and can get along with the Soviet Union." As his supporters saw it, it was Roosevelt's responsibility at Yalta to ensure that the conference was a step toward the kind of peace they desired.

The president's conservative critics—Senator Burton K. Wheeler (Dem., Montana), writer William Henry Chamberlin, and others—long had doubted that cooperation with Russia after the war would prove either possible or desirable. Many right-wing Republicans, Catholic and ethnic leaders, and conservative journalists did not want communist, Godless Russia to receive any of the fruits of victory; indeed, some of them would have been just as happy if Hitler had succeeded in destroying the Soviet state. But now that the Soviets and the Western allies clearly were moving toward military victory, Roosevelt was obliged, in their view, to do everything he could to limit Russia's influence outside its borders.

British Prime Minister Winston Churchill also faced domestic pressures, especially in regard to the future of Poland, in whose defense Britain and France had declared war on Germany 5 1/2 years before. But Churchill had the advantage of having presented to his nation a more concrete, realistic portrait of postwar world politics than American leaders had conveyed to theirs; and he also did not have as constituents millions of fairly recent immigrants from Poland and other East European nations, many of whom vehemently opposed Russian domination of the region. In addition to seeking an acceptable compromise on Poland, Churchill wanted to insure at Yalta that England's chief European ally, France, would have a zone of occupation in Germany after the war.

Marshal Josef Stalin, who had feared three years earlier that the potent German army might well conquer Russia, was in a strong position by the time of Yalta. His army, aided by U.S.

arms shipments and, since June 1944, by the Allied second front in the West, had driven the Germans all the way back from the streets of Stalingrad to the suburbs of Berlin. In the process, the Red Army had liberated Poland and other East European nations from brutal Nazi rule, and it had won for Russia the gratitude of much of the Western world. Earlier in the war, Stalin had pleaded for a large-scale second front to lessen German pressure on Russia. Now, at Yalta, it was Roosevelt who was anxious to nail down the details of Soviet assistance against Japan, and it was the president and the prime minister who were requesting Soviet concessions on Poland.

Stalin preferred the "arithmetic" of specific agreements to the "algebra" of declarations of principle, and he also believed that international relations were grounded in self-interest and the balance of power rather than in expressions of good faith or the authority of international organizations. To use the more recent language of accounting, Stalin primarily focused on the bottom line in great power politics. Although hopeful that the Grand Alliance could remain intact as long as he, Roosevelt, and Churchill remained in power, Stalin was determined that the Soviet Union would protect itself, unilaterally if necessary, against the possibility of a hostile Poland and especially against renewed German militarism. As the war neared its end, Stalin increasingly displayed what historian Vojtech Mastny[2] has called "rising aspirations" to expand Soviet power.

Contrary to the various myths about Yalta which began to develop as soon as the joint communiqué was issued on February 12, the conference itself proceeded much as one would have expected under the circumstances. The three leaders and their associates were generally cordial, as befitted successful and powerful allies who still needed each other's help to assure final victory. But they naturally bargained hard and long over dif-

---

[2] The titles, places, and dates of publication of the books of most of the historians and political scientists quoted in the text can be found in the bibliographic essay beginning on page 146.

ficult issues such as Poland, and each made numerous compromises and concessions—the Soviets on French participation
in postwar Germany, for example, and the British and Americans on leaving the Soviet-installed Lublin government as the
starting point for the future government in Poland. And where
they could not reach agreement—such as on the size of reparations from Germany—they often appointed commissions to try
to reach a solution.

Of all the issues discussed at Yalta, Poland was uppermost
in the minds of the three leaders, and it also was the most difficult to resolve. In their conversations with Stalin, Roosevelt
and Churchill eloquently expressed their concern for Polish independence. In an important meeting on February 6, Churchill
entreated Stalin to permit Poland to exercise its "sovereign independence and freedom":

I want the Poles to have a home in Europe and to be free to live their
own lives there. . . . This is what is dear to the hearts of the nation of
Britain. This is what we went to war against Germany for—that Poland
should be free and sovereign. Everyone here knows . . . that it nearly
cost us our life as a nation.

After a brief intermission, Stalin replied with equal conviction:

The Prime Minister has said that for Great Britain the question of
Poland is a question of honor. For Russia it is not only a question of
honor but of security. . . . During the last thirty years our German
enemy has passed through this corridor twice.

Despite remaining differences of interpretation on Poland
and some other issues, most of the participants considered the
conference a favorable omen for future Allied relations, and so
did the overwhelming majority of the congressmen and other
American commentators who reacted publicly to the communiqué. "By any standard, the Crimean Conference was a great
achievement," *Time* observed in its February 19 issue. "All
doubts about the Big Three's ability to cooperate, in peace as
well as war, seemed now to have been swept away." Reflecting

this positive response, a Gallup poll in late February found that 87 percent of those with opinions had a favorable impression of the Yalta Conference.

The generally positive American attitudes toward the publicized results of the Yalta Conference lasted only about three or four weeks. Both the communiqué and Roosevelt's address to Congress upon his return had implied inaccurately that the Big Three were in accord on all major issues, especially on the desirability of having elections to establish democratic governments in Eastern Europe. The results at Yalta, Roosevelt told cheering members of Congress and a nationwide radio audience on March 1, "ought to spell the end of the system of unilateral action, the exclusive alliances, the spheres of influence, the balances of power, and all the other expedients that have been tried for centuries—and have always failed."

In a vaguely worded section called the "Declaration on Liberated Europe," the communiqué had suggested that the Allies would work together to establish democratic conditions in Eastern Europe. But it in no way bound the Soviets to give up any of the preponderant leverage over the future of Eastern Europe which they had achieved as their army had swept through the region. Nor, of course, did the British and Americans even suggest giving the Russians any voice in the future of France, Italy, Greece, or other West European nations in exchange for Soviet concessions in Eastern Europe. When it became apparent by mid-March that the Russians were continuing to consolidate their position in Poland, Rumania, and elsewhere, many Americans understandably became disillusioned about Yalta. Gallup's next poll found "a marked drop-off in trust of Russia in all educational levels."

Two myths important to the development of the Cold War thus emerged in the immediate aftermath of Yalta and gradually intensified over the following five years: first, the myth that Stalin had made at the conference, and then broken, clear-cut commitments in regard to Eastern Europe and hence could not be trusted to keep his word; and second, the myth, propagated mainly by conservative Republicans, that the seriously ill and somewhat naive Roosevelt had "sold out" Poland and other American interests at Yalta. In fact, as we have seen, the Soviets at the conference never agreed to yield their dominant position in Poland; the "Declaration on Liberated Europe" was highly ambiguous; and Roosevelt and Churchill simply did not have the power—short of war with Russia—to alter the Soviet position anywhere in Eastern Europe. But there was surprise and bitterness in both America and Russia about the failure of Yalta to sustain friendly relations. Indeed, the breakdown of trust in the weeks following the conference may well be viewed as the beginning of the Cold War.

Myths about Yalta played an important role in American life for at least a decade after the conference, contributing for example to the frequent Republican charge in the early 1950s that the Democrats were responsible for "losing" both Eastern Europe and China to communism. Other myths, not always as clearly articulated or related to a single event, have also aided in perpetuating and often intensifying the Cold War.

In America there developed between the late 1940s and the late 1960s two major sets of myths, the "nationalist" and the "revisionist." Soviet leaders also developed a set of myths, and propagated them in their own country and abroad. These various mind-sets are important not only because leaders and citizens in both countries found them useful as a framework for explaining or justifying the Cold War, but also because many scholars have used portions of them as underpinnings for their writings on Soviet-American relations. The reader should remember that myth is not defined as something that is necessarily false, but rather as a belief that some people live by, often without being willing to submit it to critical examination.

Nationalist myths flourished in America between the late 1940s and the early 1960s, the height of the Cold War. Although some people did not accept this viewpoint, Americans generally agreed with statements like these:

Russia broke its wartime agreements with the West, and therefore was responsible for starting the Cold War.

Because Russia is seeking to spread communism throughout the world, America has no choice but to take firm anti-Soviet measures.

There is a monolithic international communist movement, centered in Moscow and including Communist China.

It is dangerous and a waste of time to try to negotiate with the Russians; the only thing they understand is military strength.

Democratic, prosperous America is the generous and wise leader of the Free World; communist rule, in contrast, is always unpopular and dictatorial.

During the 1960s, as liberals and radicals became fully aware of the extent of America's foreign commitments and the distortions that the Cold War had introduced into domestic life, revisionist myths gained wide exposure. These views were especially strong among young people who opposed the Vietnam War and criticized the capitalist system. Like the first set of myths, they also appeared quickly in journalistic and scholarly writing:

President Truman foolishly tried to intimidate Stalin with the atomic bomb and sought to drive the Soviets out of Eastern Europe; the United States, therefore, was primarily responsible for starting the Cold War.

America's primary goal in world affairs is economic expansion; it props up numerous right-wing dictatorships in order to protect U.S. investments.

Partly as the result of the lucrative alliance between the Pentagon and defense contractors, America is largely to blame for the wasteful and potentially disastrous arms race.

Russia's goals—peace, improved living conditions, etc.— are similar to those of other countries; communist ideology has been vastly overrated as an influence on Soviet policy, either domestically or internationally.

Like Americans viewing the world through their own values and experiences, Soviet leaders often have allowed their views of the West to be shaped by their own history and ideology. Several of their myths have contributed to misperceptions and animosity on both sides:

The capitalist nations are determined to "encircle" the Soviet Union and ultimately to overthrow its communist government.

Despite the long record of capitalist hostility toward them, the Soviets have consistently pursued a policy of "peaceful coexistence" toward the West.

A small elite, centered in Wall Street, controls the American economy and government, and hence directs U.S. foreign policy.

Marxist-Leninist "laws of history" demonstrate that capitalist nations are undergoing a process of inevitable decline, and communism is the wave of the future.

This listing of myths which have contributed to the Cold War is meant to be suggestive, not definitive. Equally important ones come readily to mind. The point in mentioning them is to underscore how vital one-sided perceptions have been in magnifying mutual distrust between the two sides—and, within the United States, between opposing schools of thought.

Perhaps the most persistent and destructive tendency in all countries involved has been to see events from the narrow perspective of one's group, rather than making the effort to understand events from the other side's viewpoint as well. An obvious example, present almost daily in most American and all Russian mass media and in political speeches, is to view one's own military spending and alliance-building as defensive and thoroughly justified, while viewing the weapons and alliances of the adversary as threatening. One reason for what Akira Iriye calls "the fundamental importance of images in relations among peoples" is the continuing influence of nationalism and ethnocentrism in shaping perceptions of other nations.

As citizens of the contemporary world, where the often intense rivalry between America and Russia has been at center stage for more than a generation, all of us bring at least some preconceptions to this subject which even a preponderance of contrary "facts" might not alter. Especially in regard to Soviet and Chinese policies, where the available documentation is much more sketchy than it is for the United States, it is well to recall French writer Michel de Montaigne's aphorism, "Nothing is so firmly believed as what we least know."

The goal of this brief, analytic book is not to judge which side was "right" and which was "wrong," but rather to assist in understanding how the Cold War emerged in the 1940s; how the attitudes and policies on both sides contributed to the Cold War's intensity in the 1950s and early 1960s; how a significant improvement in East-West relations occurred between 1963 and 1972, only to move toward renewed animosity thereafter; how, in short, the dilemmas and realities facing our present world developed, and what, if anything, that experience might suggest about our current options. In the aftermath of the Soviet invasion of Afghanistan and the Reagan administration's quest for superiority in the nuclear arms race, the issues raised by the Cold War are as relevant today as they were forty years ago.

CHAPTER ONE

Downward Spiral During the Truman-Stalin Years, 1945–1953

One way to look at Soviet-American relations during the nearly eight years between the death of Franklin Roosevelt in April 1945 and the departure of Harry Truman and Josef Stalin from power in early 1953 is to emphasize the tremendous influence

Truman, Stalin, and their like-minded associates exerted on international relations during these years. In this view, derived from the "great men" theory of history, one could note that the United States and the Soviet Union, taken together, held more power in world affairs immediately after World War II than any two nations in recent history. One also could observe that Stalin and Truman had immense personal authority over their nations' foreign policies at this time—Stalin ordered a communist coup in Czechoslovakia in 1948, for example, and Truman sent American troops to fight in Korea in 1950 without bothering to ask Congress for a declaration of war. One could even believe, as many Americans did at the time, that Stalin personally was responsible for starting the Cold War; or conversely, that Truman overreacted to limited Soviet actions in Eastern Europe and was himself largely to blame for the downturn in relations. In the early postwar years more than a few American liberals were saying, in effect, "If only Roosevelt had lived, this bitterness in Soviet-American relations would not have developed."

A contrasting approach is to argue that these were years when, in Ralph Waldo Emerson's famous words, "things are in the saddle, and ride mankind." Adherents of this viewpoint might acknowledge that American and Russian leaders affected some specific developments, but they would argue that the general course of history at this time was virtually foreordained. As the only remaining great power on the Eurasian landmass after the defeat in World War II of both France and Germany, the Soviet Union naturally expanded its influence after the war west toward Germany and east toward Japan. And the United States, the world's greatest economic and military power at the time, naturally sought to limit Soviet gains and hence reestablish the balance of power—on terms as favorable to itself as possible—in Europe and Asia. According to those who view the Cold War as virtually inevitable, the intense rivalry between America and Russia probably would have occurred even if the one had not been a capitalist nation desiring a favorable climate for trade and investments, and the other had not been ideologically committed to the expansion of communism.

Those emphasizing the importance of circumstances in explaining the origins of the Cold War might note not only the situation in 1945—including the extraordinary economic and political collapse of Europe and East Asia—but also the fairly consistent pattern of hostility in Soviet-American relations between the Russian Revolution in 1917 and 1941, the traumatic experience of both nations in dealing with Hitler's Germany after 1933, and the peculiar role that each nation had played in world politics before the 1940s. Both America and Russia were, from the European perspective, inexperienced powers; both had recent histories of relative isolation and generally bumpy and inconsistent relations with the rest of the world; and leading elements in both nations assumed the superiority and universal applicability of their own domestic institutions. In the confused new circumstances of 1945, only one fact was indisputable: the larger nations of western Europe, which had dominated world politics for several centuries, no longer were the leading actors on the international stage.

Although most readers probably will have a preference, it is not necessary to favor one of these frameworks for interpretation at the expense of the other. On the contrary, it is quite possible to suggest that circumstances conducive to a Cold War atmosphere were extremely potent, but at the same time the conduct of foreign policy in both Washington and Moscow frequently exacerbated the situation. In sum, things were in the saddle, but up there with them were frequently shortsighted and edgy leaders.

The World After the Hurricane

Herman Wouk entitled one of his best-selling novels on World War II "The Winds of War." As Wouk noted, the winds of change did blow through American life, increasing permanently the influence of such institutions as the federal government and large corporations and creating enlarged expectations in such economically disadvantaged groups as blacks and women. Succeeding the dismal depression of the 1930s, the war ushered in thirty years of economic growth. It also restored the American people's pride in their values and way of life, and virtually demolished the earlier belief that the United States could remain "isolated" from troubling events in Europe and Asia. Although tragic for those who lost sons or husbands, World War II is generally remembered by Americans who lived through it as one of their country's finest hours.

Compared with the relatively gentle breezes that reached America's shores, the winds of war which pounded Europe and Asia from 1939 to 1945 were like a six-year-long hurricane. A sizable proportion of the cities on the great Eurasian landmass and its two adjoining island-nations—Britain and Japan—were damaged severely. London was hit repeatedly early in the war by German bombers, and later in the war by German rockets. Rotterdam and other cities in the Netherlands were bombed mercilessly in 1940. Berlin was pummeled by Allied bombers until, as American diplomat Robert Murphy observed, "the odor of death was everywhere"; other German cities, like Dresden and Stuttgart, were fire bombed until tens of thousands of the residents were charred beyond recognition.

To the east, fierce fighting virtually leveled thousands of cities and towns in Eastern Europe, Russia, and China, and a concerted American bombing campaign against Japan in the last years of the war turned large areas of the compact Japanese population centers into rubble. Estimates of war-related deaths in all the countries involved run as high as 55 million, of whom roughly 20 million were Russians. The approximately 150,000 persons killed by the atomic bombs dropped on Hiroshima and Nagasaki in August 1945, therefore, represented well under 1 percent of the war's fatalities.

Despite its fearful losses in population, in wrecked cities and factories, and in destroyed dams and livestock, the Soviet Union emerged from the war with substantially increased power. Although it lacked the overall economic and military strength of the United States, it was better situated to take advantage of the vacuum of power on the Eurasian landmass resulting from the war. Whereas the United States was three thousand miles from Europe and twice as far from Asia, Russia bordered on numerous nations in Europe, the Middle East, and Asia, including such Cold War trouble spots as Poland, Hungary, Turkey, Iran, China, and Korea. As a consequence of the defeat of Germany and Japan, the respected Red Army was located in 1945 in Eastern Europe (including the eastern third of Germany), in northern Iran, and in occupied territories in the Far East. At the same time, the American and British armies were occupying equally substantial territory in Western Europe, the Mediterranean, and the Far East. The vacuum was being filled.

"This war is not as in the past," Stalin commented in a conversation with Yugoslav leaders in April 1945. "Whoever occupies a territory also imposes on it his own social system . . . as far as his army can reach. It cannot be otherwise." The opposing view, strongly held by many in the U.S. State Department at the end of the war, was summed up in a message from Roosevelt to Stalin the previous fall: "In this global war there is literally no question, political or military, in which the United States is not interested."

Although these two quotations oversimplify the evolving positions on both sides, they do suggest the broad outlines of the open conflict that developed in the immediate postwar period. With Stalin's Russia reluctant to abandon its dominant position in several neighboring nations, and with Truman's America reluctant to concede Soviet hegemony anywhere, the stage was set for the Cold War.

The Mutually Induced Breakdown of Relations, 1945–1946

Beginning with the post-Yalta acrimony in March and April 1945, Soviet-American relations deteriorated gradually and fitfully during 1945, and then more sharply and steadily after the turn of the year. Occasionally productive negotiations between the two sides continued in the Council of Foreign Ministers from the fall of 1945 until Secretary of State James Byrnes resigned in early 1947. But there could be no doubt that Truman intended to pursue a tough anti-Soviet policy after he attended Winston Churchill's famous "iron curtain" speech in Fulton, Missouri, in March 1946, and especially after he publicly fired Secretary of Commerce Henry Wallace that September, after Wallace made a speech urging greater American cooperation with Russia. So sharply had the once favorable public attitudes toward the former ally dropped by then, that Truman could count on strong public and congressional support for his decision to fire the controversial liberal.

The breakdown of Soviet-American relations in 1945 and 1946 resulted from a potent combination of issues, images, and personalities dividing the former allies. In addition, domestic political factors, bureaucratic considerations, and America's special relationship with England helped to establish what Stalin called the "two camps."

Of the major issues in dispute, none was more bitter than that of Eastern Europe, which Stalin clearly believed had been settled in his favor in negotiations before and during the Yalta Conference. Neither Roosevelt nor Truman accepted Stalin's viewpoint, however, and neither was willing in 1945 to cede most of the countries in the region to Soviet control. Shortly before he died, Roosevelt wrote letters to Stalin which criticized Soviet policy in Eastern Europe, and Truman denounced Soviet actions in Poland in a meeting with foreign minister V. M. Molotov on April 23. A believer in Woodrow Wilson's ideal of national self-determination, Truman tried numerous tactics, including a proposal for the internationalization of the Danube River and hard bargaining over peace treaties for Rumania and Bulgaria, to weaken Russian influence in the region.

In the early postwar period Stalin did not insist on subservient governments in all of the East European nations—Hungary was relatively independent internally until 1947, and Czechoslovakia until 1948. But because he viewed Eastern Europe as vital to Russia's security, the Soviet leader was determined to prevent any nation in the region from entering into an economic or military alliance with the West. By the late 1940s, handpicked leaders were installed by means of political purges and show trials of dissidents, until most of Eastern Europe, including all six countries that would form the Warsaw Pact, were fully subservient to Stalin.

Another frequently acrimonious issue involved policy toward defeated Germany. During the war American official thinking on this issue had been confused and contradictory, wavering between a desire to impose a harsh peace that would end once and for all the threat of German militarism, and a desire to rehabilitate Germany as the cornerstone of future European prosperity. Russia, having suffered the most at the hands of Germany, was determined to keep it as weak as possible, partially by forcing it to pay substantial reparations in order to help rebuild Soviet industry.

At Yalta, the Soviets won American agreement "as a basis for negotiations" of $20 billion in reparations from Germany, half of it to go to them. At the Potsdam Conference of the Big Three in July 1945, the Soviets pressed their demands for $10 billion in reparations, largely to be collected in the industrialized western zones. But Truman and Byrnes, convinced of the need to rebuild German industry, refused to agree to a dollar figure on reparations for Russia and suggested that the Soviets could remove whatever equipment they could locate from their own zone in the east.

The American leaders did allow the Russians a small percentage "of such industrial capital equipment as is unnecessary for the German peace economy," but this vague agreement meant little in practice. Russian leaders complained that Western leaders had repudiated the spirit of Yalta and shown insensitivity to their legitimate needs for recovery. The failure at Potsdam to develop a common policy on Germany facilitated the gradual evolution of two Germanies, one allied with the West and one with the Soviet Union.

A third area that contributed to tensions, especially in 1946 and 1947, related to the "Northern Tier" countries: Greece, Turkey, and Iran. This was a region of traditional Anglo-

Russian rivalry, with the United States becoming increasingly involved as it assumed the role of the economically weakened British. Due to internal instability, increasing importance as a source of oil, and proximity to important trading routes in the Middle East, all of these countries offered an inviting target for great power machinations. Russia had long wanted a guaranteed outlet through the Dardanelles Straits to the Mediterranean, and national minorities in the mountainous regions in easten Turkey and northern Iran were susceptible to Soviet influence. Moreover, Stalin did not see why the West should claim exclusive rights to Iran's huge oil reserves. Finally, despite Stalin's acceptance of Britain's dominant position in Greece, the right-wing Greek government was engaged in the early postwar period in a bitter guerrilla war against communist-led opponents supplied by Yugoslavia and other nations to the north.

In the view of some American leftists, Stalin callously abandoned the Greek rebels in exchange for British concessions in Eastern Europe. While Greece was in fact an example of Stalin's emphasis on pursuing Russia's self-interest rather than always supporting leftist movements abroad, the rebels still were able to mount a strong campaign against the British-backed government.

The first public Cold War crisis occurred in March 1946 in regard to Iran. When the Iranian government refused to grant Russia an oil concession equal to that given Britain, the Soviets supported a revolt in northern Iran and refused to withdraw their troops, as scheduled, on March 2. Byrnes, whom Truman privately and others publicly had labeled as "soft" on Russia, now moved forcefully to demonstrate his resolve. On March 5 he sent a virtual ultimatum to the Soviets demanding the removal of their troops, informed the press of his strong stand even before receiving a reply from Moscow, and encouraged Iran to take the issue to the U.N. Security Council. After hearing of alleged Russian troop movements, Byrnes angrily told an associate, "Now we'll give it to them with both barrels."

Even though the Soviets declared in late March that their army was leaving Iran, Byrnes refused to remove the issue from the agenda of the U.N. Security Council. A week later, Russia and Iran announced an agreement on the Soviet troop withdrawal, coupled with oil concessions for Russia. After the Russian troops were withdrawn, Iran, with American support, reneged on the oil agreement and settled firmly into the Western sphere of influence.

Fourth, economic issues other than those relating specifically to Germany and Iran separated Russia and the West. Needing to rebuild their economy and at the same time arguing that they could help to prevent unemployment in the United States after the war, the Soviets in January 1945 requested a $6 billion loan at low interest. The request stirred debate within the administration, but Russia received no answer at either Yalta or Potsdam. In August the Soviets requested a $1 billion loan from the Export-Import Bank, but the State Department stalled on the issue, finally telling the Russian chargé in Washington in February 1946 that the loan request was "one of a number of outstanding economic questions" between the two nations. By then relations had cooled so markedly that the administration almost certainly could not have obtained congressional approval for a loan even if it had asked for one. Russia, for its part, chose not to join the two American-dominated organizations designed to ensure postwar prosperity, the World Bank and the International Monetary Fund.

Another important issue involved Soviet-American rivalry in East Asia, especially in regard to Japan and China. At Yalta, Stalin had won territorial concessions from Japan—notably the Kurile Islands and the southern half of Sakhalin Island—but Russia never achieved an effective voice in the occupation of Japan. "I was determined that the Japanese occupation would not follow in the footsteps of our German experience," Truman recalled. "I did not want divided control or separate zones." Soviet leaders negotiated vigorously in the early postwar period to try to increase their influence on Japan's reconstruction, but to no avail. Although American unilateralism in postwar Japan angered Stalin, there was little, short of war, that he could do about it.

Under the leadership of General Douglas MacArthur, the United States dominated Japan, transforming the former enemy into a close and increasingly prosperous ally. Over Soviet objections, the United States and fifty other nations signed a peace treaty with Japan in September 1951, and in a separate security treaty the United States insured that its armed forces and weapons could continue to be deployed there. As the American scholar Edwin O. Reischauer noted in 1950, "Our position there is not very different from that of Russia in the smaller countries of Eastern Europe, however dissimilar our motives may be."

To put it mildly, American policy was not as successful in China. Truman and most other American leaders wanted China to continue to be an ally of the United States, but they recognized that Chiang Kai-shek's Nationalist government was corrupt and might not be able to win the long-standing civil war with the Communists, led by Mao Tse-tung. Partly for its own reasons and partly because of pressure from Republicans, the Truman administration briefly sent fifty thousand U.S. troops to North China in 1945 and continued to send substantial military and economic aid to Chiang's government through 1948. At the same time, especially during General George C. Marshall's mission to China in 1946, American leaders urged Chiang to negotiate a compromise settlement with Mao. Sporadic negotiations between the two sides failed, and by 1948 the Communists clearly were winning the civil war.

Frustrated by America's "failure" in China, conservative critics blamed Roosevelt for "selling out" China at Yalta and demanded that Truman take stronger measures to try to prevent a Nationalist defeat, but Truman refused in 1948 and 1949 to send American troops. While some Americans blamed Russia for Chiang's difficulties, Stalin had given only modest aid to Mao and indeed was ambivalent about whether he even wanted the Chinese Communists to win the civil war. The reality was that the Chinese themselves—not America or Russia—would decide their nation's future.

The last major issue—clearly the most portentous one—was policy toward atomic energy. America and Britain, as in many things, worked together closely during the war to develop the atomic bomb. Despite some feeling in the government that Russia should be let in on the secret in order to lay the framework for cooperation on atomic energy in the postwar era, the Soviets were not informed until after the first bomb was tested in New Mexico in July 1945.

Upon hearing the news of the successful blast at the Japanese city of Hiroshima on August 6, which killed roughly eighty thousand people, Truman remarked to an associate that "this is the greatest thing in history." In a radio address explaining the significance of what had happened, the president reported deceptively that "Hiroshima, an important Japanese Army base," had been destroyed. A few days after another Japanese city, Nagasaki, was decimated on August 9, the war in the Pacific came to an end, and America's use of atomic weapons appeared vindicated.

Truman's decision to drop atomic bombs on densely populated Japanese cities without explicit warning was controversial within the government and the scientific community at the time, and it has been debated vigorously by historians ever since. Recent, careful studies of the issue by Martin J. Sherwin and other scholars have concluded that Truman did not use the weapons primarily to intimidate Russia, as some writers had charged, but rather that the decision resulted more from the momentum of bureaucratic decision-making on the subject and from the assumption that any weapon available should be used to convince the "fanatical Japs" that continuing the war was futile, and thus avoid a costly invasion of Japan. By 1945, few high officials had moral scruples about bombing civilians.

Whatever the precise role of Soviet-American relations in Truman's decision to use atomic weapons, Stalin was apprehensive about America's possession of them. Germany, with its technological superiority, had come close to defeating Russia earlier in the war, and now Russia, despite its great victory, faced even greater insecurity. In mid-August a concerned Stalin reportedly told a high-level meeting in the Kremlin: "A single demand of you, comrades: Provide us with atomic weapons in the shortest possible time. You know that Hiroshima has shaken the whole world. The equilibrium has been destroyed. Provide the bomb. It will remove a great danger from us."

The hardening of Soviet policy, evident at the Foreign Ministers' meeting in September and in other actions that fall, may well have been related in part to the intense anxiety apparent in Moscow after Hiroshima and Nagasaki. Joseph G. Whelan has observed that throughout modern Russian history, and especially during the early Cold War period, the Soviets have acted aggressively in negotiations when they have believed they have had to compensate for their actual weakness. After meeting with people close to the Soviet leadership, Averell Harriman, the American ambassador in Moscow, wrote Secretary of State Byrnes in November that the sudden appearance of the bomb "must have revived their own feeling of insecurity." Harriman noted that "the Russian people have been aroused to feel that they must again face an antagonistic world. American imperialism is included as a threat to Russia."

Given the enormous complexity of the issues involved in atomic energy and the deepening Cold War atmosphere, it was highly unlikely that the United States and Russia would have been able to agree in 1946 on international control of atomic energy and hence have prevented an atomic arms race. Nevertheless, the Truman administration made an effort, however flawed, in that direction. A carefully drafted study, directed by Dean Acheson and David Lilienthal, was completed in March. With sufficient trust and a willingness to compromise on both sides, this proposal for an international agency to control both raw materials and production plants for nuclear weapons might have formed the basis for at least a limited agreement. But by the time Bernard Baruch took the greatly altered proposal to the United Nations in June and told the Soviets they would have to accept his entire proposal or get nothing, the Russians blocked the proposal, denounced it as a disguise for a permanent U.S. atomic monopoly. The United States, in turn, rejected Russia's proposal that existing stocks of nuclear weapons be destroyed. Both nations thus continued their substantial nuclear programs, leading in 1949 to the first successful Soviet test and, in the early 1950s, to the decision by each government to develop the vastly more destructive hydrogen bombs.

The nuclear arms race quickly became a central feature of the Cold War, distinguishing the Soviet-American rivalry from other great power conflicts in the past. Nuclear weapons both set limits to the struggle—that is, helped to keep it cold—and also intensified it in many ways, not the least of which was the fear in each country that the other might try to obliterate it in a surprise attack. Even at those times in which there have been relatively few other major issues in dispute, the threat of nuclear destruction has loomed like a thunderhead over Soviet-American relations.

These six major issues—and other lesser ones, such as the status of Korea—tended to separate Russia from America and Britain in the early postwar period. All of these issues posed genuine and difficult dilemmas for both sides; they were not merely pretexts for animosity. They all grew out of the war and of Germany's conquest in Europe and Japan's in Asia; they thus had their origins well before Truman replaced Roosevelt in April 1945 and Clement Attlee replaced Churchill as Britain's Prime Minister that July, and should not be viewed primarily as the consequence of inexperienced leadership. Given the intractability of the issues and the intensity of emotions on both sides as early at 1946, the leaders of Russia and the West deserve credit for maintaining at least the semblance of peace in Europe for more than a generation after World War II. Their behavior in Asia had more tragic consequences.

Although numerous images harmful to Soviet-American relations flourished in the late 1940s (including many mentioned in the Prologue), perhaps the most important ones on the American side were the Munich analogy and the myth of American virtue; and, on the Russian side, the myth of inevitable capitalist-imperialist hostility, contributing to an obsessive fear of their own weakness, and the view that only they could ensure their own security. Within a year after the war there began to develop what have been called mirror-image official viewpoints: Russia (or, as seen from Moscow, the United States), with its threats and growing armaments, was pushing the world toward war.

The Munich Conference of 1938, where the British and French caved in to Hitler's demand for western Czechoslovakia in the hope of maintaining peace, was a powerful symbol to many Americans of the dangers of appeasing an unscrupulous dictator. Ernest R. May and other historians have noted how deeply this analogy affected the thinking of leading American policy-makers after the war, and how many tended to view Stalin as another Hitler bent on world domination. This was also the thinking of literally thousands of editorialists, radio commentators, politicians, business and labor leaders, clergy, and others who influenced popular opinion on foreign policy issues.

Stalin often was ruthless in defense of what he perceived to be Soviet interests in the areas he controlled. But, as his pullback from Iran in 1946 should have suggested, he was not reckless and certainly did not initiate war, as Hitler did. "The image of a Stalinist Russia poised and yearning to attack the West, and deterred only by our possession of atomic weapons," diplomat George Kennan observed a decade later, "was largely a creation of the Western imagination." The Munich analogy, in short, not only clouded American perceptions of world affairs; it also infuriated the Russians, who viewed comparison with the hated Nazis as an almost unspeakable obscenity.

The other vital image in understanding American attitudes and behavior was the myth of unusual virtue and superiority to other nations, what historian T. H. Von Laue has called "unconscious ethnocentric arrogance." This was simply the view, reinforced strongly by the nation's involvement in World War II, that the United States was the hope of the world both in its wondrous internal institutions and in its selfless commitment to world peace, justice, and prosperity. An intensive public opinion survey in the summer of 1946 found that only 15 percent were satisfied with the current state of international relations, and most of the rest blamed Britain and, especially, Russia. "Their own country, on the other hand, seemed to them to be trying steadfastly to achieve justice and harmony," the public opinion analysts concluded. "It was, if anything, too generous with its material goods, and too lenient toward those governments which place obstacles in the road toward these goals."

As Stalin allegedly was following in Hitler's footsteps, so Truman, many Americans felt, was bringing to fruition the noble ideals of Woodrow Wilson and Franklin Roosevelt. Even those Americans who did not like Truman's policies still envisaged their nation as the world's virtuous leader. Critics as diverse as Wallace and conservative Senator Robert Taft (Rep., Ohio), for example, agreed with the president that America had a unique and noble destiny. This proposition, while accepted with reservations by many West Europeans grateful for American assistance against the Nazis and in postwar recovery, obviously was not considered self-evident in Moscow.

In increasingly virulent official statements in *Pravda* and elsewhere, the Soviets also trumpeted the superiority of their system and its eventual triumph over decadent capitalism. At the same time, they insisted that the West was preparing to attack Russia in order to destroy their way of life. This second image more accurately reflected their feelings of insecurity, their technological inferiority in the military and other sectors, and their growing isolation in world affairs. Their isolation, in turn, was intensified by their vitriolic propaganda, their frequent rudeness and deviousness in diplomatic gatherings, their brutal suppression of dissent in Eastern Europe, and their highly publicized spying in the West. While these measures may have been necessary in their view to ensure their security, they may well have lessened the Soviets' actual security by inspiring alliances against them. As both nations were to discover (but not necessarily to learn) several times during the Cold War, an obsession with security may actually decrease it and lead to the brink of war.

Nor did the personalities of the Soviet and American leaders contribute to less hostile relationships between the two nations in the postwar period. A communist revolutionary before the Bolshevik triumph in 1917, Stalin had known the harsh realities of being raised by a drunken father and being subjected to imprisonment and exile. Whether or not these youthful experiences were decisive in shaping his character as a ruler, the fact remains that, during his twenty-five years in power, he ordered the summary execution of millions of his countrymen and confined millions more to the horrible gulags, or concentration camps, of which Alexander Solzhenitsyn has written so eloquently.

Fearful that even his closest associates might betray him, Stalin did not hesitate to order the murders of capable and experienced military and diplomatic officers, leaving a decimated officer corps to lead the Russian defense against Germany in 1941 and a youthful and narrowly-trained diplomatic corps to handle Russia's new responsibilities after 1945. "He saw enemies everywhere," his daughter commented later. Although he did not view Roosevelt in this light, it seems clear that Stalin viewed Truman with strong suspicion by the time of the Soviet leader's first sharply anti-Western speech in February 1946.

Truman had enjoyed a much more normal youth, a positive experience as an officer in the American armed forces in France during World War I, and, after a failure in business, a successful career in local and national politics. Known primarily as a staunch Democrat and as a critic of waste in defense procurement during World War II, Truman had never been considered a Senate expert on foreign affairs. His tendency to equate Stalin's Russia with Hitler's Germany was epitomized in a public remark just after Germany attacked Russia in June 1941: "If we see that Germany is winning, we ought to help Russia and if Russia is winning we ought to help Germany and that way let them kill as many as possible. . . ."

Stunned by Roosevelt's sudden death and lacking knowledge and experience in world affairs, Truman had gotten off to a shaky start in Soviet-American relations. But the new president soon steadied his course and came to be known, in contrast to Roosevelt, for his well-organized administrative style and his willingness to make clear-cut decisions. Truman also won the gratitude of State Department officials for restoring much of the authority and importance in foreign affairs which they had lost under FDR. Much more skeptical of Russia during the war than the White House and the military, the State Department (except for the relatively conciliatory Byrnes) now was able to exert strongly anti-Soviet influence on the new president.

Although Truman's positions on substantive issues probably were more important, some features of his personality contributed to the downturn in relations with Russia. Perhaps to make up for his inexperience in diplomacy, Truman could be cocky and cold in negotiations, particularly in comparison with his smooth, ingratiating predecessor. The president also tended to see issues in black-and-white terms, which often gave his speeches on foreign affairs, his diplomatic notes, and his private comments a tinge of the self-righteousness and superiority so common in the public discourse of those years. "I knew at Potsdam that there is no difference in totalitarian or police states, call them what you will, Nazi, Fascist, Communist or Argentine Republics," Truman wrote his daughter Margaret at the time of the Truman Doctrine. Like Stalin, Truman by early 1946 was comfortable with the idea that the other superpower was best viewed as an adversary. In international politics such images, when held at the highest levels, quickly become translated into realities.

Finally, what role did public opinion and Congress play in the shift toward Cold War in 1945 and 1946? My own analysis, contrary to that of some recent writings, holds that Truman and his advisers were affected by the sharp downturn in public attitudes toward Russia in late 1945 and early 1946, and that the way the administration handled the Iranian situation, for example, had a definite domestic political component. This was also the case in the firing of Wallace later that year, which occurred partly to ward off Republican charges of appeasement during the 1946 Congressional elections and to preserve Republican Senator Arthur Vandenberg's support for a hard-line, bipartisan foreign policy.

A careful study of editorial coverage in Texas in the fall of

1945 found strong hostility toward Russia, and in Connecticut, another state in which attitudes have been studied closely, Polish-Americans, Italian-Americans, and Republican politicians were bitterly anti-Russian by late 1945. Research on the news media consistently has shown that stories featured on the front page and in broadcasts are ones emphasizing the news values of confrontation, conflict, and controversy. Sharp criticisms of Russia and of domestic communists, regardless of whether they were substantiated by facts, were staples of page-one stories, magazine articles, and radio broadcasts throughout the Truman-Stalin years. No matter how firm the administration became toward Russia and toward domestic communists, many Americans viewed it as being on the defensive and not responding adequately to the communist threat.

In the American system presidents—especially ones new to the office—are politicians before they are statesmen, and Truman, faced with high inflation, strikes, and other serious domestic problems, could not afford to run the risk of being labeled as an "appeaser" in American relations with Russia. The president had grasped this point by early 1946, as Secretary of State Byrnes could well attest. While Byrnes, after a tongue-lashing by Truman in January 1946, was allowed to continue to negotiate with Russia, he was instructed to emphasize a strong anti-Russian stand in his public statements. In this case, Truman clearly was affected by strong pressures from large segments of the press and from Republicans in Congress to take a harder line toward Russia.

It is true that, as the Cold War developed, the administration was responding to the almost universal anti-Russian sentiment which its own anti-Soviet statements and policies had helped to solidify. But both the public and the press throughout these years had numerous sources other than the administration on policy toward Russia, and these were largely hostile to Moscow as early as the fall of 1945. In the absence of strong and consistently conciliatory signals from Moscow, it was only natural that a beleaguered administration, already inclined toward a tougher stance, would embrace the widespread and growing anti-Soviet sentiment in the nation and try to turn it to its own political advantage.

Containment and Counter-Containment, 1947–1949

The events that signaled the enunciation of a definite American policy of "containment" of the Soviet Union occurred in rapid-fire succession in a crisis atmosphere from February through July of 1947. The spark that set off the chain reaction inside the government was the British message to the State Department, delivered on February 21, that, because of internal economic difficulties, Britain would have to stop giving military and economic aid to Greece and Turkey as of March 31. Top officials—already concerned about Western Europe's economic problems, accentuated by severe weather—quickly agreed that the United States would need to assume Britain's role in order to prevent the spread of Soviet influence in the region. The problem was to convince an economy-minded, Republican-controlled Congress to make prompt and substantial commitments to these countries.

In a meeting with congressional leaders at the White House on February 27, Truman, newly installed Secretary of State George Marshall, and other officials presented their case. When Marshall's low-key presentation failed to sway the congressmen, Acheson asked to speak. The influence of the democracies in world affairs had been declining ever since the end of the war, Acheson declared, while the Soviet Union had been expanding its influence. If Greece or Turkey now fell, Asia, Africa, and the Middle East would be open to Soviet penetration. Moreover, Soviet ideology was implacably hostile to the West, and the division of the world was more profound than at any time since the ancient rivalry between Rome and Carthage. Failure to act thus would create a grave threat to American security. "Mr. President," a shaken Senator Vandenberg said when Acheson had finished, "if you will say that to the Congress and the country, I will support you and I believe that most of its members will do the same."

On March 12, before a joint session of Congress and a nationwide radio audience, Truman did just that. The president did refer to the situation in Greece and Turkey, and he did ask for $400 million in aid for the two nations. But in the best-known part of the speech he sweepingly divided the world in two and, in what became known as the Truman Doctrine, pledged American assistance to the "free peoples":

At the present moment in world history nearly every nation must choose between alternative ways of life. The choice is too often not a free one.

One way of life is based upon the will of the majority, and is distinguished by free institutions, representative government, free elections, guarantees of individual liberty, freedom of speech and religion, and freedom from political oppression.

The second way of life is based upon the will of a minority forcibly imposed upon the majority. It relies upon terror and oppression, a controlled press and radio, fixed elections, and the suppression of political freedoms.

I believe that it must be the policy of the United States to support free peoples who are resisting attempted subjugation by armed minorities or by outside pressures.

As Henry Wallace and some other commentators pointed out afterward, the governments the United States would be supporting in Greece and Turkey were a far cry from the ideal represented in Truman's speech. Even some within the administration, such as George Kennan, considered the apparent commitments in the speech much too imprecise and far-reaching. But Truman's approval rating in public opinion polls increased from 49 percent in January to 60 percent in late March, and the percentage viewing foreign policy issues as the most important facing the nation shot up from 22 percent in December to 54 percent in March. Despite grumbling from some congressmen who believed that they had no choice but to approve the aid measure now that the president had staked American prestige on it, the Senate approved by a vote of 67 to 23 in late April, and the

House concurred in early May by 287 to 107, with solid Republican as well as Democratic majorities in favor. With the Cold War in full swing for the following fifteen years, both Democratic and Republican presidents could count on strong congressional support, especially when military spending was involved.

In his commencement address at Harvard University on June 5, Secretary of State Marshall made a general offer of economic aid to Europe in order to facilitate "the revival of a working economy in the world so as to permit the emergence of political and social conditions in which free institutions can exist." This led to the development of the Marshall Plan and the eventual expenditure of more than $12 billion in economic aid, which proved invaluable in restoring the economies of Western Europe and earned the enduring gratitude of millions of citizens of the nations involved. Not entirely altruistic, the Marshall Plan led to large orders for goods in the United States and to greatly increased American trade and investment in Europe. Unwilling to accept the strings inevitably attached by American oversight of the program, the Soviet Union declined to participate, and forced its satellites to do likewise.

The final highlight of this period of intense activism in American foreign relations was the appearance, in the July issue of the prestigious journal *Foreign Affairs,* of an article entitled "The Sources of Soviet Conduct" and written by "X" (soon identified as Kennan). In an administration short on experienced and knowledgeable students of Soviet behavior, the articulate, scholarly Kennan emerged by early 1946 as the leading U.S. government expert on Russia. Called home from Russia that year and installed by the spring of 1947 as head of the State Department's Policy Planning Staff, Kennan provided theoretical underpinnings for American policy in the early postwar period.

Given the Cold War atmosphere, it is not surprising that most of his higher-ranking colleagues paid more attention to his scathing indictments of the Soviet system and its alleged tendency toward expansionism than they did to his calls for restraint and balance in American policy. The "X" article, which first used the word "containment" to describe American policy toward Russia and which was the most famous of Kennan's writings, focused on the evils of Soviet communism and urged "a long-term, patient but firm and vigilant containment of Russian expansive tendencies" to be achieved, in part, by the "application of counter-force at a series of constantly shifting geographical and political points."

In the first volume of his memoirs, published in 1967, Kennan regretted his "failure to make clear that what I was talking about . . . was not the containment by military means of a military threat, but the political containment of a political threat." Regardless of what Kennan may have wished he had included, the "X" article as written clearly contributed to the deepening hostility toward Russia in 1947 and 1948.

Moving beyond the often self-righteous rhetoric, what did containment mean in practice between 1947 and 1949? Contrary to the warlike language of Truman's speech to Congress, before 1950 it did not mean a global anti-communist crusade, but rather a more limited one in which distinctions between vital and peripheral interests were made. While recognizing the tendency of even the most carefully conceived policy to bend with events, five overarching trends seem clear:

1   Definite economic and military commitments abroad, but limited primarily to Europe, the Middle East, and Japan. Within Europe, the greatest emphasis was given to increasing the strength of the western zones in Germany, which in May 1949 became the Federal Republic of Germany.

2   The limiting of defense spending to what Truman believed the nation could afford (about $12–14 billion per year), leading to an emphasis in military planning on nuclear weapons—still a U.S. monopoly—to deter possible Soviet attacks.

3   Open support for any communist nation willing to break with Moscow (e.g., Josip Broz Tito's Yugo-

slavia), and covert support (e.g., through activities of the Central Intelligence Agency, established in July 1947) to opponents of Stalin within Eastern Europe.

4   An unwillingness to send unlimited American aid to forestall a Communist victory in the civil war in China, despite pleas from right-wing Republicans and others to "save Chiang."

5   An apparent unwillingness to explore seriously with Russia possible areas of compromise in regard to major European issues (e.g., Germany).

While most of these themes of American strategic thinking in the late 1940s are fairly self-explanatory, the last one requires elucidation. Because high American officials normally did not test seriously the occasional Soviet offers of negotiations on major issues between 1947 and 1953, it is difficult to judge the Russian leaders' sincerity. In the spring of 1947, for example, Stalin gave a highly friendly interview to Governor Harold Stassen of Minnesota and, in the Council of Foreign Ministers meeting in Moscow, had Molotov suggest renewed bargaining on Germany.

Adam B. Ulam, an expert on Soviet foreign policy, believes that Stalin might have been willing to accept a unified, non-communist Germany in return for increased reparations to Russia (a perennial Soviet request), the continued demilitarization of Germany, and Western recognition of Poland's postwar borders—a deal which, in Ulam's view, would have been in the West's interest to accept. Stalin also hinted strongly to Secretary of State Marshall the need for a summit meeting with Truman. But Western leaders were suspicious of Soviet intentions, and Marshall reported upon returning to Washington that no progress had been made on major issues.

After the failure of the Moscow talks, there was very little serious negotiating on major East-West issues during the remainder of the Truman-Stalin years. Although Soviet officials deserve their share of the blame for tensions during these years, it is also true that Marshall and his successor, Acheson, interested as they were in denouncing Soviet behavior and in creating "situations of strength" prior to serious negotiations, contributed to the ominous breakdown of East-West diplomacy after 1947. "There is only one language they understand, force," Truman remarked to an associate in 1949. As historian Alonzo L. Hamby has noted, "The president and his subordinates celebrated American superiority, engaged in self-righteous stubbornness toward the Soviet Union, and clothed even their most constructive proposals in the garments of American mission and destiny."

Stalin in 1947 and 1948 demonstrated that hard-nosed containment was a game two could play. Denouncing the Truman Doctrine and Marshall Plan as a capitalist offensive against his rule, the Soviet dictator took steps which, from his viewpoint, contained the West. The non-communist, elected Hungarian leader, Ferenc Nagy, was removed from office in May 1947; and, in a move that shocked Western opinion, Soviet collaborators overthrew the elected Czechoslovak government in February 1948. Czech leaders had made the mistake of agreeing to accept aid under the Marshall Plan, a move quickly squelched by Moscow, but one which nevertheless had proved their "unreliability." Both the mysterious death in early March of Czech Foreign Minister Jan Masaryk, a friend of the West, and the implausible explanation that he had committed suicide by jumping out of a window, symbolized for many the brutality of Stalinism. By confirming the apparent wisdom of Truman's hard-line stance, the events in Czechoslovakia dealt a severe blow to the independent presidential campaign of Henry Wallace, who now looked more like an unthinking apologist for Russia's policies than an intelligent critic of America's.

The Berlin crisis of 1948–1949 provided another excellent example of the reciprocal nature of containment. Just as the Marshall Plan appears to have played a part in precipitating the events in Czechoslovakia, so Allied steps toward organizing a separate West German state and introducing a new currency for West Germany apparently led the Soviets to impose, by late June of 1948, a complete blockade of all surface routes through eastern Germany to West Berlin, which since the war had remained an enclave under the three Western powers' control inside East Germany. An outpost of relative economic prosperity and political freedom more than one hundred miles inside the Soviet sphere, West Berlin was, as Nikita Khrushchev later put it, a "bone in the throat" of Russia. Fearing above all else a strong and rearmed West Germany, Stalin apparently believed that the blockade would force the West to negotiate with Russia a settlement of the German issue as a whole.

If that was indeed Stalin's reasoning, he made a serious error, for Truman by this time obviously was not going to accommodate Russia, especially not under duress during an uphill presidential campaign. The president responded with a massive and continuing airlift of supplies to the more than two million West Berliners and the Allied personnel stationed there. Although tensions frequently ran high, neither side wanted war: Stalin kept channels for negotiation open, and Truman did not force the issue of Western surface access rights to Berlin. After negotiations in Moscow failed by late August, the tendency in Washington was to forget about negotiating with Russia and step up planning for a formal Western military alliance, established in April 1949 as the North Atlantic Treaty Organization (NATO), and for a West German state, led by the staunchly anti-Communist Konrad Adenauer.

By November 1948 Kennan was concerned about the West's "general preoccupation with military affairs, to the detriment of economic recovery and of the necessity for seeking a peaceful solution to Europe's difficulties." In retrospect, this concern seems largely justified. But it must be added that Stalin's moves were themselves contributing to the increased militarization of Western policy that the Soviet leader so greatly feared. And it also should be pointed out that, after Czechoslovakia and Berlin, the administration clearly was acting in accord with public sentiment. The respected Survey Research Center of the University of Michigan reported in October 1948 an "almost unanimous belief that Russia is an aggressive, expansion-minded nation," and noted an "overwhelming demand for firmness and increased 'toughness' in relations with Russia . . .''

Their blockade having failed either to isolate Berlin or to change Western policy elsewhere in Germany, the Soviets in early 1949 signaled their interest in ending this dangerous stalemate. With normal diplomatic channels impaired, Stalin on January 30 used his reply to a question by journalist Kingsbury Smith to suggest the possibility of fruitful negotiations. With the United States then taking the initiative, secret discussions took place in February and March between the Deputy American Representative to the U.N. Security Council, Philip C. Jessup, and his Soviet counterpart, Jacob Malik. After significant Soviet concessions, on May 5 an announcement was made that the blockade would be lifted on May 12 and that a Council of Foreign Ministers meeting focusing on German issues would convene in Paris on May 23. Although the United Nations had failed in the years since 1945 to live up to the hopes of its founders, it had thus proved its worth as the locus for delicate and important international negotiations.

When Acheson returned to Washington in late June after the completion of the Council of Foreign Ministers meeting, he was, according to *Time's* lead story in its July 4, 1949, issue, "pleased but not complacent." According to Acheson, since 1947 "the position of the West has grown greatly in strength, and that . . . of the Soviet Union in regard to the struggle for the soul of Europe has changed from the offensive to the defensive." In his statement concerning the meeting, Truman emphasized that Britain, France, and the United States had shown great unity in dealing with the Russians.

From their viewpoint, the president and the secretary of state had reason to be pleased with overall developments in Europe since those hectic days when the Truman Doctrine was being formulated in early 1947. Buoyed by substantial American support, the Greek government gradually had defeated the insurgency, and both Greece and Turkey had become members of the Western alliance. Austria, while still occupied by Russian as well as Western troops, clearly was tilting toward the West. The Marshall Plan had strengthened the economies of most West European nations, including France and Italy, whose communist parties had failed in their bid for power. Compared with eastern Germany, the western zones already were an economic and political showcase, and Berlin had become a symbol of Western determination to stand up to the Russians.

Even in Eastern Europe, Tito had broken with Stalin in 1948, and he was showing definite signs of being able to maintain his independent course, in part because of U.S. economic aid. Covert CIA activities, some successful in literally destroying supporters of Stalin, were underway on a substantial scale in Eastern Europe, and Radio Free Europe and Radio Liberty were beaming the Western propaganda line behind the "iron curtain." More seriously, political repression and economic difficulties were sapping the vitality of East European nations. In the Cold War in Europe between containment and counter-containment, the West was more than holding its own.

Significantly, the *Time* article which had begun by praising Acheson's work in Europe ended by denouncing the administration's policy in Asia. After reporting that twenty-one senators had criticized "the bankrupt U.S. policy toward China," the influential magazine concluded: "Time, and the Russian tide, were working against the Western nations in Asia. What had to be done had to be done fast." Much to the dismay of *Time* and of many other Americans, the Communists finally won the Chinese civil war that fall, and Chiang Kai-shek fled to the island of Taiwan. And to the surprise and dismay of administration officials, Russia exploded its first atomic bomb that September. Compared with the excitement and enthusiasm of early 1947, the Cold War, like some earlier shooting wars, was getting nastier and less manageable with each passing month.

The Most Dangerous Phase, 1950–1952

Of all the years between the end of World War II and the present, 1950 stands out as the most fateful in terms of America's stance in the Cold War. Before the year ended, the United States had more than tripled its defense budget, it was openly aiding Chiang Kai-shek on Taiwan and the French in Indochina, it was fighting North Korean and Communist Chinese troops in Korea, it had committed itself to the rearmament of West Germany and the stationing of more than four divisions of its own troops in Western Europe, it was moving rapidly to develop the hydrogen bomb, and it was negotiating for new bases in Spain and elsewhere.

In congressional testimony in regard to NATO on April 27, 1949, Secretary of State Acheson had assured concerned senators that "the disarmament and demilitarization of Germany must be complete and absolute," that the United States did not plan to send a large number of troops to defend Europe, that the administration was not contemplating security agreements with other nations, and that membership in NATO did not imply acceptance of European colonialism. Partly as the result of opportunities and dangers created by the Korean War, the administration by the end of 1950 reneged on all of these assurances.

The early 1950s were the most dangerous phase of the Cold War, not because of the Korean War in itself, but rather because of what the Korean War confirmed: namely, that both sides, prisoners by now of the Cold War tendencies to miscalculate and to think the worst of the other's intentions, were prone to tragic errors of policy. It also was highly dangerous because, in the wake of the Communist victory in China in October 1949, neither America nor Russia had a clearly formulated policy in Asia, as events quickly confirmed. Whereas both sides' vital interests in Europe had been largely delineated by the summer of 1949, neither side was able, even in the early 1950s, to develop a coherent, workable strategy toward Asia. If ever there was an experience that demonstrates the dangers of blocking the channels of effective communication and proceeding on the basis of ideology, dubious assumptions, and domestic pressures, this period was such a time.

Many of the errors of American policy during the last years of the Truman administration appear, at least in general terms, in National Security Council Paper Number 68, one of the most significant documents of the Cold War. Prepared under the leadership of Paul Nitze, Kennan's hawkish replacement as head of the Policy Planning Staff, the secret NSC-68 called for an American-led offensive against Soviet influence in the world. Viewing communism as monolithic, the policy report called for a firm response to communist aggression anywhere and in whatever form it might appear; it also suggested that the United States should work to remove Russian power from Eastern Europe, a policy proposal which soon came to be known as "rollback" or "liberation."

"The assault on free institutions is world-wide now, and in the context of the present polarization of power a defeat of free institutions anywhere is a defeat everywhere," the report noted ominously. Responding to the Soviet explosion of its first atomic bomb, NSC-68 argued that the Soviets might be able to launch a powerful attack against the West by 1954. "The Soviet Union is developing the military capacity to support its design for world domination," it asserted. To meet the communist threat, the report urged a vast increase in American defense spending, stepped-up covert activities, and other actions to increase the nation's power and that of its allies.

Although NSC-68 was completed in April 1950, Truman did not approve it until that September, three months after the outbreak of war in Korea. By then its hard-line conclusions appeared highly plausible, especially to those who viewed the Korean War as just one step in the Kremlin's "design for world domination." Like a few officials at the time, most historians today view NSC-68 as alarmist in its description of Soviet intentions and mistaken in its assumption of a monolithic communist bloc. Using recently declassified sources, Samuel F. Wells argues that the officials who drafted NSC-68 exaggerated the Soviet military threat to the West. In a classic example of acceleration of the arms race, the resulting American military buildup apparently contributed to a substantial increase in Russia's defense effort.

Even before the Korean War, the administration was moving away from Kennan's original emphasis on containment of

Russia to the NSC-68 emphasis on opposing communism wherever it might appear, even if it was based on an indigenous revolutionary movement against a repressive or colonial government. In so doing, it was making two tragic errors of policy, one in regard to China and the other in regard to Vietnam. In China the administration was moving toward the decision, cemented in stone by the Korean War, to continue to treat Chiang Kai-shek's regime as the sole government of China even after it had lost control of every Chinese province except Taiwan, and to have no relations with Mao Tse-tung's government on the mainland, which actually ruled the overwhelming majority of Chinese. This was especially regrettable because, as late as the summer of 1949, the Chinese Communists had raised the possibility of developing ties with the United States as a counter balance to Soviet influence in China. But the administration, fearing an adverse domestic political reaction led by the fervently pro-Chiang "China Lobby" in Congress and in the press, refused to let its envoy in China talk directly with Mao, and it declined to recognize the new government that fall.

Although Acheson in his policy address to the National Press Club in January 1950 recognized in theory the importance of nationalism in limiting Soviet influence in Asia, in practice he quickly came to treat Mao as an agent of Russian imperialism. With the Chinese Communists responding to the American rebuffs with hostile actions of their own (such as raiding the American consulate in Peking and trumpeting anti-American propaganda), twenty years of bitter Sino-American hostility had begun by the spring of 1950.

Whereas in its China policy the key issue was whether the administration could accept the Communist victory in the civil war and encourage China's traditional nationalistic rivalry with Russia, in its policy toward Vietnam the dilemma was whether to support French colonialism or Asian nationalism. Because the United States historically had stood for self-determination and because Roosevelt had opposed the reinstatement of European colonialism in Asia after World War II, it might appear that this would have been an easy choice in favor of the Vietnamese. In the eyes of administration leaders, it definitely was not. Vietnam's drive for independence from France was led by Ho Chi Minh, a communist trained in Moscow in the 1920s, whereas France played a pivotal role in Acheson's plans for a united, militarily strong Western Europe.

On a visit to Paris in May 1950, therefore, Acheson acceded to France's long-standing request for military and economic aid in Indochina. "The United States Government," Acheson declared in his fateful announcement which marked the first step in the ever-increasing American involvement in Vietnam during the 1950s and 1960s, "convinced that neither national independence nor democratic evolution exist in any area dominated by Soviet imperialism, considers the situation such as to warrant its according economic aid and military equipment to the Associated States [French-sponsored governments in Indochina] and to France." As with Mao Tse-tung's desire to maintain his independence from Moscow, the situation was doubly unfortunate because Ho Chi Minh in the mid-1940s had begged the United States to assist Vietnam in establishing its independence from both France and China.

Even more than in its China policy, the administration was permitting its obsession with the evils of communism to cloud its thinking. Although he was a communist, Ho was also a nationalist determined not to become subservient to either Moscow or Peking. "It is better to sniff French dung for a while than eat China's all our life," he once observed in a comment reflecting Vietnam's traditional hatred of Chinese domination. The administration's error lay not in failing to support Ho, which hardly could have been expected in the anti-communist atmosphere of the late 1940s and early 1950s, but in attaching itself to French colonialism, which was highly unpopular throughout Asia. As George C. Herring has concluded, "Regardless of his ideology, Ho by 1950 had captured the standard of Vietnamese nationalism, and by supporting France, . . . the United States was attaching itself to a losing cause."

In fairness to Truman and his advisers, it should be noted that the decision to aid the French in Vietnam did not appear to be momentous at the time, and that the administration's decision to continue to support Chiang Kai-shek evolved only gradually, much slower than many domestic critics of the administration would have liked. Indeed, the "loss" of China unleashed an often vicious barrage of criticism against the administration for its alleged foreign policy failures. The bipartisanship which had dominated foreign policy decisions in Congress from the passage of the aid to Greece and Turkey in 1947 through the acceptance of American participation in NATO in the summer of 1949 was at a low ebb. The Democrats were losing the Cold War, critics like Richard Nixon (Rep., California) and Kenneth Wherry (Rep., Nebraska) charged. The administration was doing too much in Europe and too little in Asia, Robert Taft (Rep., Ohio) insisted, and it was spending far too much money for the meager results it had been achieving. Such charges apparently were having an impact: the United States was falling behind in the Cold War, a plurality of respondents were telling the pollsters, and Russia was winning.

For better or worse, accusations by leaders of the opposition party that the administration in office is losing the Cold War have been a recurring feature of American political rhetoric from the late 1940s to the present. What was different in this highly dangerous phase of the Cold War was that, in addition, Senator Joseph McCarthy (Rep., Wisconsin) and others were charging that high administration officials were traitors to their country, that at least some of the major foreign policy developments of the late 1940s resulted from disloyalty to the United States.

This reckless attack, which others started well before McCarthy discovered the publicity to be gained from it, was given credence by the arrest and conviction of several people on charges of spying on the American atomic energy program, and especially by the charge in 1948 that Alger Hiss, an official in the State Department under Roosevelt, had been a Soviet spy during the 1930s. The charges and countercharges relating to the Hiss case made headlines all through 1949, and on January 21, 1950,

Hiss was convicted of perjury in connection with testimony before the House Un-American Activities Committee. On February 9, McCarthy made the first of his sensational, never-substantiated charges that there were large numbers of communists in the State Department.

The sharp attacks on Truman's foreign policy and on the loyalty of high officials (including Acheson, Secretary of Defense George Marshall, and even General Dwight Eisenhower) helped to keep the administration on the defensive during the remainder of the president's term. Apparently seeing political gain, responsible Republican leaders refused to criticize McCarthy and the others who were trafficking in innuendo and fear, and the president's sharp criticisms of McCarthy tended to be dismissed as self-serving. The result of the anti-communist hysteria and the denunciation of the nation's leaders was a virtual no-win situation for Truman: no matter how strongly he opposed Stalin, Mao Tse-tung, Ho Chi Minh, and the other "Communist devils," he could never do enough to satisfy his critics.

The vocal right-wing critics of the administration were especially vehement in their denunciations of Acheson, whose resignation or firing was demanded repeatedly after the Communist victory in China, and again after the outbreak of the Korean War. In his National Press Club address in early 1950, Acheson had reiterated the administration's position that the American "defensive perimeter" ran from Alaska to Japan and then south to the Ryukyu Islands and the Philippines. Those friends of the West living on the mainland of Asia would need to depend first upon their own efforts and then "upon the commitments of the entire civilized world under the Charter of the United Nations." After Russian-backed North Korea began its invasion of American-backed South Korea on June 25, Acheson's critics were quick to blame him for the attack on the grounds that he had given North Korea the green light by not including South Korea in the line of defense. Acheson, a lawyer before becoming a statesman, sought to defend himself by citing his reference to U.N. commitments and by noting that the United States took the lead, through the U.N., in coming to South Korea's defense.

Why did the North Koreans attack? The best account of the immediate circumstances leading to the attack is contained in Nikita Khrushchev's memoirs, published in 1970. According to Khrushchev, Kim Il Sung, the Soviet-trained North Korean leader, asked Stalin at the end of 1949 to approve an attack on the South to unify the country under Kim's leadership. Recognizing the possibility of American intervention, Stalin hesitated and asked Kim to think it over carefully and, if still committed, to draw up detailed plans for the invasion. When Kim did this and when Mao Tse-tung also approved, the Soviets "wished every success to Kim Il Sung and toasted the whole North Korean leadership, looking forward to the day when their struggle would be won." Although the Russians supplied and trained the North Korean forces, they largely avoided direct military involvement in the conflict.

Stalin's approval of the invasion, if not its timing, is far more certain than his reasons for doing so. Many American officials assumed at the time that the attack was but the prologue to a more general Soviet offensive. This assumption helped to justify the administration's successful request to Congress for greatly increased military expenditures, but it always has lacked supporting evidence. Citing substantially more evidence, Kennan argues that unilateral American steps toward a peace treaty with Japan in early 1950—including permanent American bases there—may have triggered Stalin's response. Others, also avoiding the common contemporary view that Stalin was just another Hitler, have argued that, after the United States had avoided direct military intervention in China, had withdrawn its forces from South Korea in mid-1949, and had suggested that Korea was outside its defensive perimeter, Stalin may well have concluded that the United States would not intervene in a civil war in Korea. Finally, given the almost complete breakdown of Soviet-American relations and mounting evidence of American "encirclement" of Russia, the coldly realistic Stalin may have seen little to lose in permitting the North Koreans to cause trouble for the United States.

And why did the Truman administration respond so decisively to a situation which might have been viewed as a civil war between Koreans? Here the documentation is ample. "If this was allowed to go unchallenged it would mean a third world war, just as similar incidents had brought on the second world war," Truman later remembered thinking as he rushed back to Washington to plan the American response. "It was also clear to me that the foundations and the principles of the United Nations were at stake unless this unprovoked attack on Korea could be stopped." Truman, who vividly recalled the 1930s and was sensitive to the attacks on the administration for its "weakness" in Asia, never hesitated to act forcefully in this situation. Indeed, if any communist leaders genuinely thought that he would do otherwise, they were sadly misinformed about both the president and the political climate in which he operated. Truman received strong support for military action from his cabinet, from leaders of both parties in Congress, from the press, and from public opinion polls. He also received a lucky break when, due to Russia's continued boycotting of the U.N. Security Council for its failure to seat the new government in mainland China, the administration was able to conduct its military operations against North Korea under U.N. auspices.

Just as the Soviets would have been pleased to have Korea united under Kim Il Sung, so leading American officials, viewing the North Korean government as unrepresentative, had long desired the unification of the country according to Western principles. Accordingly, the administration did not hold for long to its original public objective in the Korean War—driving the North Koreans out of South Korea and restoring the 38th parallel as the boundary between the two sides. Instead, under pressure from the American commander, General Douglas MacArthur, and from some officials in Washington, the administration by August had decided to try to destroy the North Korean army and unite the area under South Korean leadership. Areas held by North Korean forces were hit repeatedly by devas-

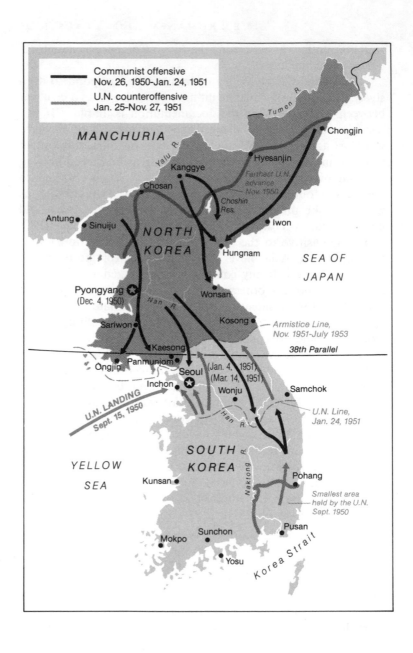

Communist offensive
Nov. 26, 1950–Jan. 24, 1951

U.N. counteroffensive
Jan. 25–Nov. 27, 1951

MANCHURIA

Tumen R.

Chongjin

Yalu R.

Kanggye

Hyesanjin

Chosan

*Farthest U.N.
advance
Nov. 1950*

*Choshin
Res.*

Antung •

• Sinuiju

NORTH
KOREA

• Iwon

Hungnam

SEA OF
JAPAN

Pyongyang ✪
(Dec. 4, 1950)

Nan R.

Wonsan

Sariwon •

Kosong •

*Armistice Line,
Nov. 1951–July 1953*

• Kaesong

38th Parallel

Ongjin • Panmunjom •

Seoul ✪

(Jan. 4, 1951)
(Mar. 14, 1951)

Inchon •

Wonju •

• Samchok

Han R.

*U.N. Line,
Jan. 24, 1951*

U.N. LANDING
Sept. 15, 1950

SOUTH
KOREA

Naktong R.

YELLOW
SEA

Kunsan •

• Pohang

*Smallest area
held by the U.N.
Sept. 1950*

Mokpo •   Sunchon •

Pusan

• Yosu

Korea Strait

tating bombing raids and artillery and naval fire, all of which resulted in heavy military and civilian casualties in both parts of Korea. Militarily, the situation was beginning to look favorable for the American side.

Whereas the North Koreans and Soviets had miscalculated in June, by early autumn it was the Americans who were overplaying their hand. Ignoring suggestions for a ceasefire at the 38th parallel and disregarding repeated warnings by the Chinese that they would feel compelled to join the fighting if the Americans came too close to their territory, U.N. forces invaded North Korea in September and October and bombed bridges on the Yalu River between North Korea and China. Contemptuous of the Chinese Communists and friendly to Chiang Kai-shek, MacArthur assured Truman on October 15 that, in his opinion, the Chinese would not risk becoming involved. When large numbers of Chinese soldiers did attack across the Yalu in late fall, the Americans, who had seemed close to total victory in Korea, were forced to fall back rapidly toward the 38th parallel.

MacArthur now asked for permission to carry out massive air strikes against China, but officials in Washington, wishing to avoid a wider and more dangerous war, denied his request and ordered him to concentrate on stabilizing the U.N. position near the 38th parallel. When MacArthur in the spring of 1951 publicly implied that Truman was an appeaser and disobeyed orders by crossing the 38th parallel again, the president, backed strongly by the joint chiefs of staff, fired him on April 11. Still viewing Russia as enemy number one and the defense of Western Europe as the top priority, General Omar Bradley, the chairman of the joint chiefs, told Congress that an all-out war in Asia would be "the wrong war, at the wrong place, at the wrong time, and with the wrong enemy." In a relatively brief period the administration, as Barton J. Bernstein has noted, had gone from containment to liberation and then back to containment.

With the outspoken MacArthur gradually fading from public view and the front in Korea stabilized by late spring, officials in Washington and the Far East, in Acheson's words, "found themselves united on political objectives, strategy, and tactics for the first time since the war had started." In other words, the administration was ready to try to negotiate a settlement. Following the pattern of the Berlin negotiations of 1949, Kennan met secretly with Malik twice in early June, and learned that the Soviets were interested in ending the hostilities. After Malik publicly affirmed Russia's interest in a peaceful solution on June 23, the administration moved rapidly to make contact with the Chinese and North Korean commanders, and formal negotiations began on July 10. Although an armistice agreement was not signed until July 1953 (partly due to America's refusal to give up the lands it held north of the 38th parallel and to return Chinese and North Korean prisoners of war against their will), the intensity of the fighting subsided sharply from the previous level.

Frustrated by the lack of a peace agreement, Truman wrote in his journal on January 27, 1952, that "the proper approach now would be an ultimatum . . . informing Moscow that we intend to blockade the China coast from the Korean border to Indochina . . . ," and that "if there is further interference we shall eliminate any ports or cities necessary to accomplish our peaceful purposes." The president mentioned several Russian and Chinese cities (including Moscow and Peking) which would be destroyed, presumably by nuclear weapons; fortunately, Truman acted contrary to his private musings, as his firing of MacArthur and his restraint in Korea in 1951 and 1952 show.

In the absence of a peace agreement, Truman's popularity, which had taken a nose dive after Chinese intervention dashed hopes for an early victory, never recovered to its July 1950 level. Republicans, smelling victory in 1952, jumped on inconsistencies in American policy in the Far East and played on the popular feeling that all America was getting in Korea was military casualties and higher taxes. In a Gallup poll in April 1951, 66 percent disapproved of Truman's firing of MacArthur, and that October 56 percent responded that Korea was a "useless war." On the other hand, the public strongly approved the keystones of America's Cold War stance: hostility toward Russia and mainland China, large defense expenditures, production of hydrogen bombs, rearmament of Germany, a strong American military presence in Europe, American bases in Japan, and support for Chiang Kai-shek. Truman might not have been able to win an election for dogcatcher in 1951 and 1952, but his vision of America as the assertive leader of the "Free World"—the vision of NSC-68—was more solidly embedded in public thinking than ever before.

The depth to which Soviet-American relations had dropped was illustrated by Kennan's experience in 1952 as the American ambassador to Russia. On the American side, Kennan was sent to Moscow without instructions from his own government. Accordingly, he did not seek an appointment with Stalin, for, "being effectively without instructions, I had nothing to say to him." On the Soviet side, Kennan was shocked by the "viciousness and intensity" of the anti-American propaganda that spewed forth daily from the Russian news media. The American embassy was bugged, and he felt like a prisoner in his official residence. Although he believed that Soviet charges against the United States were greatly exaggerated, he did believe that American military activities in Europe and in the Mediterranean were at times unnecessarily provocative: "I began to ask myself whether . . . we had not contributed, and were not continuing to contribute—by the overmilitarization of our policies and statements—to a belief in Moscow that it was war we were after."

While traveling through Germany that September, Kennan carelessly stated that current conditions in Moscow were worse than he had experienced in Berlin in the early 1940s. Infuriated by Kennan's implicit analogy of Russia and Nazi Germany, the Soviets refused to let him reenter the country, thus ending his brief tour as ambassador. In doing this, ironically, they were closing the door on one of the very few high-level American officials of that era who could see both sides in the Cold War.

Conclusion

What conclusions emerge from the early post–World War II period, the years in which the East-West division between "communism" and "freedom" developed its basic geographical outlines? At various times fairly simple conclusions have been reached: that the United States courageously stood up and accepted the "responsibilities of world leadership" in response to a Soviet challenge of global scope; or, conversely, that Truman embarked on a comprehensive Cold War crusade far exceeding what was warranted by actual Soviet policy.

As I have implied, I believe that any overall assessment of either Soviet or American policy during these years is likely to be misleading, and that one must make careful distinctions in evaluating the particular policies and attitudes on both sides. One can credit the effort represented by the Marshall Plan to assist European nations in improving their economies, while at the same time questioning the usefulness and propriety of CIA efforts to undermine governments in Eastern Europe. Similarly, one can recognize Stalin's caution in grudgingly accepting Yugoslavia's independence or in keeping Soviet forces out of Korea after the United States began to seek victory there, and yet doubt the necessity of the harshness with which he often operated in Eastern Europe. In evaluating Cold War events, one first must make the effort to comprehend the actual viewpoints of the opposing sides. Unfortunately, this basic principle of diplomacy was falling into disuse in both Washington and Moscow in the late 1940s and early 1950s.

An underlying reason why leaders in both capitals often ignored the other side's viewpoint was because of the huge cultural gap separating the two nations. America had a largely open, pluralistic society, with a tradition of considerable individual and journalistic freedom and compromise among interest groups. Americans tended to feel comfortable dealing with people with similar cultural backgrounds, notably West Europeans. Russia, in contrast, had a largely closed, totalitarian society, whose basic institutions and values were vastly different from those in the West. At the risk of overgeneralization, it seems fair to say that, partly because of this cultural gap, Soviet leaders often misinterpreted the reasons for particular American actions abroad; and American leaders, for their part, often operated on the premise that the communist government in Russia was illegitimate because it was dictatorial and, in American eyes, totally lacking in popular support. And if Stalin's rule was illegitimate in his own country, it followed that the extension of Soviet power beyond Russia's borders also lacked legitimacy. As Kennan's experience in 1952 illustrated, Russian leaders were highly sensitive to suggestions that their system, like Hitler's, was undeserving of international respect.

Two final conclusions about the early Cold War years stand out: first, hostility on one side breeds hostility on the other, and the risk of miscalculation and war thus grows unless both sides work to brake and then reverse the downward spiral; and, second, adopting hard-line policies against the other superpower in particular situations is at least as likely to trigger a hard-line response as it is to elicit moderate behavior. Although some of the trends of the early Cold War period may have been virtually unavoidable at a time of newly predominant American and Russian power and tough-minded leadership in Washington and Moscow, the tendency toward rigidity and self-righteousness in both governments was an unfortunate legacy of the Truman-Stalin years.

CHAPTER TWO

The Institutionalized Cold War, 1953–1962

In retrospect, the decade between the coming to power of new leaders in both the United States and Russia in early 1953 and the Cuban missile crisis in late 1962 has several unifying themes. One is an increased desire for improved relations among the highest-ranking leaders on both sides—notably Premier Nikita S. Khrushchev and President Dwight D. Eisenhower—limited by their own Cold War assumptions, by their mutual reluctance to make the substantive concessions required to reach agreement on important issues, and by the continued hard-line stance of many of their own advisers and of others with influence in their societies. A second theme is expanded official and nonofficial contacts between the two sides, contributing to an overall decline in tensions to a level below that of the last Truman-Stalin years. A third theme is the recurrence of some issues which had been important in the early years of the Cold War, such as the still unresolved German question and problems created by the nuclear arms race. A fourth theme is the spreading of the Cold War to nations previously untouched by direct Soviet-American competition—Laos, Egypt, the Congo, Cuba, and others—all of which, from the American viewpoint, were within the Western sphere of influence. Many of these developing nations were emerging from European colonial rule, and therefore lacked experience in self-government. Their political instability, their need for economic assistance, and their potential strategic value in the East-West competition all made them targets for idealistic and self-serving involvement by the two superpowers.

Despite some modest improvements in relations, therefore, the combination of potentially catastrophic issues and Cold War methods of operation resulted in frequent periods of tension reminiscent of the late 1940s and early 1950s. Having become institutionalized during the Korean War with large bureaucracies and industries on both sides dedicated to waging it, by the late 1950s the Cold War looked as if it might last forever.

On the communist side, this decade belonged largely to Khrushchev and, to a much lesser degree, to Mao Tse-tung. After a period of collective leadership following Stalin's death, Khrushchev emerged by 1955 as the top Soviet leader, but still a man subject to constraints and pressures from others in the Kremlin much more than Stalin had been. Having risen from his peasant birth to a high position under Stalin, Khrushchev possessed qualities which Stalin had lacked: affability, an enjoyment of mingling with people and of making speeches, an interest in traveling abroad and meeting foreign leaders, and a concern about the popularity of his government both at home and abroad. Khrushchev could be rude and threatening, as when he angrily took off his shoe and beat it on the table at the United Nations in 1960, but Westerners who dealt with him at least felt that they were dealing with a genuine, approachable human being.

Mao, in contrast, largely remained in China and focused on transforming this populous nation into a communist state based more on his own ideals than on the Soviet model. Mao's able associate, Chou En-lai, usually represented Chinese interests abroad. Kept out of the United Nations and other international forums largely by the United States, China broadcast diatribes against Western imperialism and threatened Chiang Kai-shek's government on Taiwan. Although some American leaders and intelligence analysts were aware by the early 1950s of tensions in Sino-Soviet relations, most politicians and commentators, committed to the concept of a unified Sino-Soviet bloc, tended to discount this rift until it became unmistakable in the early 1960s.

On the American side, the moderate Eisenhower and his hard-line secretary of state, John Foster Dulles, contributed the most to policy-making during the 1950s, and President John F. Kennedy had the greatest influence in 1961 and 1962. In the wake of the Vietnam War and Watergate, Eisenhower's historical reputation has grown considerably, and he is now frequently viewed as a president more interested in lessening Cold War tensions than in waging an unremitting struggle against international communism. While there is considerable validity in this interpretation, it runs the risk of being carried too far. Eisenhower often was quite cautious in his response to Soviet initiatives on Cold War issues, and he pursued a vigorous policy of containing Russian and Chinese influence. Although it is now known that Eisenhower maintained personal control of policy on major issues, it often appeared at the time that he had delegated his authority to the experienced and articulate Dulles, and to his equally hard-line brother, CIA director Allen Dulles.

And just as there has been some tendency to underestimate

Eisenhower's commitment to the Cold War, Kennedy's frequently has been overstated. Although the young, activist president supported direct U.S. involvement in guerrilla wars and greatly increased defense spending at a time when America already had a substantial strategic advantage, he was willing to seek improved relations with Russia and, apparently, even with China. Moreover, the major issues he faced in his first two years in office—Laos, Vietnam, Berlin, Cuba, the role of the CIA, arms control, and others—were bequeathed to him, in ominous form, by the Eisenhower administration. This point is made not to exonerate Kennedy of all errors, but rather to note the pronounced continuities between Eisenhower's last years and Kennedy's first two, which together form the second dangerous phase in Soviet-American relations.

The Cold War at Home

Before proceeding to discuss in more detail the diplomacy of the 1950s and early 1960s, it seems appropriate to focus briefly on the domestic context of the Cold War in the United States, the atmosphere which would have made it difficult to shift policy toward Russia and China abruptly even if it had been possible diplomatically to do so. In focusing on the United States, I am not suggesting that there were no domestic constraints on policy in Russia and China. On the contrary, it can be argued that "vigilance against imperialism" served as an important justification for limiting freedom of expression and enforcing sacrifices in Eastern Europe and North Korea as well as in the two major communist nations. It also seems clear that important elements of the national security establishment in Moscow—like their counterparts in Washington—came to have a stake in continued hostility; and that political leaders in Moscow and Peking—as in Washington—used attacks on the "correctness" of rivals' views on foreign policy as a means of wresting power from them. But while the effects of the Cold War may have been equally profound in some communist countries, they were more visible in America's largely open society, with its tradition of free expression, profitable defense industries, and elections to reward or punish politicians in power.

One other caveat is required at this point: what follows is not intended primarily as an indictment of Cold War America, but rather as an effort to provide information about some of the effects of the Cold War on the nation's life. The excesses which I describe generally were byproducts of the American people's attempt to adjust to the nation's bewildering new role of superpower. They were not, on the whole, sinister schemes concocted by malicious officials or private groups. The threat of nuclear war was frightening. The "burdens of world leadership" were substantial. Communism was a threat to democratic institutions, though not to the degree that many Americans thought it was in the 1940s and 1950s. But, as some people also realized at the time, excessive anti-communism also was a threat to the nation's institutions and values, and it is this theme that I shall develop here.

Beginning in the late 1940s and continuing until the mid-1960s, staunch anti-communism was a staple of American public life. Although the practical message of McCarthyism was that everyone should demonstrate an unswerving commitment to anti-communism or risk losing his job, most Americans needed no such stimulus to convince them that Russia and China should be opposed vigorously. The Cold War consensus on this point included both political parties, labor unions, and business groups, mass circulation magazines and daily newspapers, ethnic and religious groups, veterans and professional organizations, and liberal and conservative interest groups. The American Bar Association's Standing Committee on Education Against Communism, one of the numerous committees established throughout the society to alert the public to the Red threat, warned as late as 1964 that "to mistake the illusion of peace for genuine peace would be a profoundly dangerous, perhaps fatal mistake," and that, because "the clash between our two systems is . . . irreconcilable, then our victory will not be achieved until freedom and justice prevail everywhere in the world.''

Liberals like Democratic Senator Hubert Humphrey and conservatives like Republican Senator Barry Goldwater disagreed on the best means of opposing communism, but they both strongly supported anti-communism as the central thrust of U.S. foreign policy, and both consistently voted for generous appropriations for the Defense Department, the intelligence agencies, and America's allies abroad. Humphrey, the Senate's leading liberal, warned in 1955, a time of relative thaw, that ''we should not be deluded by Communist strategy. We know its objective.'' ''A tolerable peace . . . ,'' Goldwater wrote in 1960, ''must *follow* victory over communism.''

The news media also were preoccupied with this issue. The three news magazines—*Time, Newsweek,* and *U.S. News and World Report*—all took a tough Cold War stance, as did the most widely circulated magazine, *Reader's Digest.* Respected reporters like Theodore White and Charles Mohr left Time-Life Publications after their stories were repeatedly altered to reflect publisher Henry Luce's hard-line anti-communist, pro-Chiang Kai-shek viewpoint. Only slightly more conciliatory were the two most influential newspapers in Washington, the *New York Times* and the *Washington Post.* Both the newspaper with the largest circulation, the *New York Daily News,* and the largest chain, the Hearst papers, were virulently anti-communist. Widely circulated columnists like David Lawrence, Joseph Alsop, and William S. White all adamantly opposed the Russian and Chinese governments and warned repeatedly that the United States was falling behind in the Cold War.

The obsession with communism filtered down to the nation's youth. Boy Scouts were taught the communists were the enemy, parochial school students learned that communism was inherently evil because it was ''godless,'' and public school students had to memorize the ''evils'' of communism to pass civics tests. Congress pointedly added the phrase ''under God'' to the

Pledge of Allegiance, recited daily in schoolrooms across the country. When fear of atomic attack ran high in the late 1950s and early 1960s, civil defense programs were introduced into the schools. In one ludicrous but not atypical example, students at a public high school in Baltimore were taught to get down on their knees and put their heads on the seats of their desks whenever the teacher blew a whistle—as if that would somehow protect them during a nuclear attack. From the late 1940s through the early 1970s, men graduating from high school could expect to be drafted into the army and sent to serve in places like Germany, Turkey, Korea, and ultimately Vietnam. To pay these and other costs, more than 11 percent of the entire Gross National Product was devoted to defense spending in some "peacetime" years.

To be sure, some liberals opposed the drift of American policy. An occasional magazine like the *Progressive* and a few groups like the Friends Committee on National Legislation called for improved relations with Russia and recognition of mainland China. A well-organized segment of the scientific community opposed the atmospheric testing of nuclear weapons, and several liberal groups developed on this issue in the late 1950s. But overall, critics of America's Cold War stance, frequently denounced as "soft on communism," attracted meager support from the general public or from politicians. And for every liberal who actively sought a relaxation of Cold War tensions, there was a staunch conservative who demanded "victory" in the Cold War against communism.

By the mid-1950s, the bedrock of support for a strongly anti-communist foreign policy came from conservatives of both parties (mostly Democratic in the South, mostly Republican in the North and West); from ethnic groups of East European descent (concentrated in large northern cities like Buffalo, Cleveland, and Chicago); from fundamentalist Protestants and conservative Catholics; from labor unions like the AFL-CIO and their political supporters like Senator Paul Douglas (Dem., Illinois); and from people connected with the military, especially officers charged with the task of combatting communism all over the globe, contractors dependent on military procurements for much of their livelihood, and veterans proud of their service in previous wars and determined that the nation's defenses should remain strong. Public opinion studies found that men, who occupied virtually all of the leadership positions in American society at the time, consistently took a more hard-line position on Cold War issues than did women. The strength of anti-communist feeling was such that, to my knowledge, not a single senator publicly advocated a fundamental shift in policy toward Russia or recognition of mainland China between 1953 and 1962.

Analysis of the anti-communist impulse frequently focused on the influence of defense industries and the military in setting national priorities. In his farewell address on January 17, 1961, Eisenhower noted that, since World War II, the United States had created "a permanent armaments industry of vast proportions," that the "defense establishment" of the government had 3 1/2 million employees, and that defense spending exceeded the net profits of all American corporations. "In the councils of Government, we must guard against the acquisition of unwarranted influence, whether sought or unsought, by the military-industrial complex," the president warned. "The potential for the disastrous rise of misplaced power exists and will persist." Eisenhower said that the nation "must also be alert to the danger that public policy could itself become the captive of a scientific-technological elite."

Although Eisenhower's warning became a standard feature of liberal and New Left rhetoric in the 1960s, its validity has been difficult to assess. At what point, for example, does influence become unwarranted? Is the close relationship between Defense Department officials, contractors, pro-military magazines like *Aviation Week,* defense-industry lobbyists, and members of Congress compatible with the national interest, or does it fuel needless and dangerous arms competition? And even if many large corporations, labor unions, universities, and research institutions profit substantially from defense contracts, do the benefits they provide to the nation outweigh the costs? These issues involve value judgments as well as facts, but there

can be no denying Eisenhower's comment that "the very structure of our society" had been affected by the militarization of
American life since World War II.

The Cold War had other important consequences for
American institutions and values, some known at the time and
others revealed in recent years. One consequence well-known at
the time was the purging of officials who were accused of dis-
agreeing with policy on sensitive issues. Respected experts on
China like John Stewart Service and John Paton Davies were
fired from the State Department in the early 1950s for predicting
earlier that Chiang Kai-shek probably would lose the civil war in
China. J. Robert Oppenheimer, one of the nation's most distinguished atomic scientists, had his security clearance removed,
partly due to his opposition to developing the hydrogen bomb.
The message quickly spread through a demoralized State
Department and other agencies that clear thinking and independent analysis might well lead to the unemployment lines.

Little known at the time was the fact that the FBI, the CIA,
and the Defense Department, in addition to or as a byproduct of
their normal functions, were secretly abusing the civil liberties
and threatening the health of numerous Americans and Cana-
dians. The FBI, for example, conducted continuing surveillance
against civil rights leader Martin Luther King, Jr., on the
premise, never substantiated, that "Communist influence"
dominated his movement. Contrary to its charter, the CIA also
conducted extensive surveillance of individuals within the
United States, including members of Congress. Seeking to learn
to control behavior, the CIA conducted experiments with hallu-
cinogenic drugs on unsuspecting Americans, at least one of
whom committed suicide while unknowingly under the influence
of LSD. Experimenting in bacteriological warfare, the Navy in
1950 blanketed San Francisco for six days with a bacteria known
as serratia (which, it was discovered later, could cause a fatal
pneumonia). And the Army in 1953 conducted chemical warfare
tests over St. Louis, Minneapolis, and Winnipeg, Canada, dropping cadmium sulfide and zinc in aerosol clouds.

The most serious threat to the health of Americans at the height of the Cold War involved nuclear testing, which took place above ground in Nevada and in the Pacific between 1945 and 1963. During that time, an estimated 250,000 servicemen were exposed to testing at fairly close range, and thousands of civilians in nearby Utah also were exposed to radiation from the tests. An epidemiologist for the state of Utah, Dr. Joseph Lyon, testified in April 1979 that children growing up in his state's fallout areas in the 1950s suffered 2 1/2 times as much leukemia as children living there before and after the tests. The tests continued even though Atomic Energy Commission officials were aware by 1953 of the high levels of radiation hitting some Utah communities, including St. George, a town AEC chairman Lewis L. Strauss described as one "they apparently always plaster."

Less carefully studied have been the effects of the testing on the servicemen who were ordered to lie in trenches as close as thirty-five hundred yards from the spot where atomic weapons larger than those dropped on Hiroshima and Nagasaki were being detonated. During the AEC's "Operation Teapot" series of tests in 1955 and at other times, the Army was interested in learning if soldiers could survive on the nuclear battlefield; accordingly, thousands of GIs were exposed to large doses of radiation (often leading to nose bleeding and other symptoms) during the blast, and then they were ordered to march over radioactive terrain to "take" an objective closer to ground zero. Many servicemen were hospitalized as a result of this experience, and some who thereafter contracted leukemia or fathered children with gross deformities became bitter about being used as "guinea pigs" during their military service.

Another disturbing effect of the Cold War on American life was the compromising of respected private institutions to further the anti-communist crusade. The *New York Times* withheld stories (such as the secret preparations for the Bay of Pigs invasion) potentially embarrassing to the government; CBS regularly passed on information gained in newsgathering to the CIA; professors at leading American universities helped to recruit foreign students for the CIA and were paid to make trips abroad to gather intelligence; the AFL-CIO worked closely with American officials in undermining elected governments in Latin America; and missionaries, doctors, and corporate officials worked as secret agents for the CIA. When Catholic officials in the late 1970s looked into the qualifications for sainthood of the famous American medical missionary in Laos in the late 1950s, Dr. Tom Dooley, they found that he had been closely involved with the CIA's counterinsurgency work there. Although most Americans did not realize the extent of CIA involvement abroad during the 1950s and early 1960s, many in the affected nations did, thus lending some credibility to Russian and Chinese charges that most Americans abroad were CIA agents.

In sum, the America that the Cold War helped to create was so convinced of its responsibility to lead the "Free World" against communism that it made preparations for war the chief priority of the federal government, fired dedicated State Department officials, risked the lives of its own citizens in chemical and nuclear testing, and involved itself in trying to direct the internal affairs of scores of nations around the globe. Although Americans did not know everything the CIA was doing, the attentive public, members of Congress, journalists, and of course leaders of the administration knew that the CIA, under the president's direction, was involved in overthrowing the government of Iran and restoring the Shah to power in 1953, in overthrowing the government of Guatemala in 1954, and in trying to overthrow the government of Cuba in 1961. Most people did not know about serious CIA plotting in places like Laos, Indonesia, Syria, the Congo, and British Guiana, but most probably would have acquiesced as they did in the other three. And yet Americans almost certainly would have been infuriated to the point of demanding war if a foreign government had been discovered trying to overthrow the nation's government or assassinate its leaders.

Reflecting the Cold War mentality, a secret government panel reported in 1954 that the United States "must learn to subvert, sabotage, and destroy our enemies by more clever, more sophisticated and more effective methods than those used against us.'' The danger, always easier to grasp in retrospect, was that the nation might prove even more successful in subverting its own institutions and values.

A Modest Improvement in East-West Relations, 1953–1955

For approximately three years after the death of Stalin in March 1953—and the end of the Korean War that July—there occurred a limited but nonetheless significant improvement in East-West relations. The change occurred mainly in Soviet relations with the West, for the United States adamantly refused to recognize mainland China, which Dulles described as "fanatically hostile to us and demonstrably aggressive and treacherous." Eisenhower agreed that Mao Tse-tung's government was "beyond the pale"; indeed, his administration's major policy initiative in Asia was to "unleash" Chiang Kai-shek's exile government, supplied with American arms, to conduct raids against the mainland and, later, against North Vietnam. Hostile to Taiwan and to the U.S. both in word and in deed, the mainland Chinese during the Eisenhower-Dulles years provoked serious crises in regard to the offshore islands of Quemoy and Matsu in 1954–1955 and again in 1958.

So hostile and self-righteous was Dulles's view of mainland China that, when Chou En-lai offered to shake hands with him at the Geneva Conference on Indochina in 1954, Dulles brusquely turned his back on him and walked away. The next year Chou proposed at the Bandung Conference of nonaligned nations that the United States and China begin negotiations on outstanding issues. The administration initially declined, but soon meetings at the ambassadorial level were occurring in Geneva and Warsaw. Despite these contacts between 1955 and 1967, American officials continued to insist that Chiang Kai-shek was China's legitimate leader and, despite a 1957 invitation from Peking to American journalists which might have broken the ice in Sino-American relations, refused to allow journalists or other Americans to visit the mainland.

Fortunately, Soviet-American relations were considerably more positive, even though the vast majority of American officials and the public continued to believe that Russia was a mortal enemy. It could be argued, at the risk of giving Soviet leaders too much credit, that the improvements in Russia's relations with the West occurred despite Dulles's opposition and Eisenhower's hesitation; that, in other words, Russia's repeated diplomatic initiatives and occasional concessions created a momentum for achieving modest agreements which even the highly skeptical secretary of state could not withstand. Taking office on a platform criticizing containment and calling for a determined policy of "liberation" of Eastern Europe and China from Soviet rule, the new Republican administration found itself negotiating with Russia while, at the same time, continuing the Truman administration's policy of building alliances against it.

The Eisenhower administration, Adam Ulam has observed, "was well suited to counteract Soviet misbehavior, to isolate and contain a Russia of the Stalinist model. But it was ill suited to deal with *intermittent* Soviet misbehavior combined with appeals for friendship and eulogies of coexistence." Nevertheless, the new leaders on both sides were able to lessen tensions somewhat, and that in itself was a rare achievement during the fifteen years between 1947 and 1962.

The new administration's basic objective was to wage the Cold War more vigorously, more coherently, and more economically than its predecessor had done. The vigor and coherence were to come from the effort to ring the Soviet Union and China with a series of alliances, all led by the United States, while simultaneously encouraging dissension and revolt within the communist bloc and generally discouraging nonalignment and neutralism outside it. Using aid and fear of communism as lures, the United States was able to sign up several nations for the Southeast Asia Treaty Organization (SEATO), founded in 1954, and several others for the Baghdad Pact (later the Central

Treaty Organization, or CENTO), designed to protect the Middle East. In theory, the United States now had reliable allies from Norway and Great Britain (members of NATO) in the west to the Philippines and Australia (members of SEATO) in the east.

The financial savings were to come from the administration's "New Look" defense strategy, which was designed to lessen reliance on conventional forces and to favor nuclear weapons and the bombers and missiles capable of delivering them. This approach, Dulles declared, would allow the West "to retaliate, instantly, by means and at places of our own choosing," and thus keep the communists off balance. By spending less on expensive ground forces, the nation could achieve, in the parlance of the time, "more bang for a buck."

Although critics at home and in Western Europe feared that this approach might lead to nuclear war at the slightest provocation, Dulles remained vague as to precisely what means the United States would use in particular situations, and Eisenhower, as is now well known, kept a cool finger on the nuclear trigger. Concerned about the economic consequences of large defense budgets and deficit spending, the president limited military spending to roughly $40 billion per year, below what Democratic critics by the late 1950s considered necessary. One consequence of the administration's economy campaign, together with its desire not to "lose" any more nations to communism, was its emphasis on relatively inexpensive covert operations, which peaked during the 1950s and early 1960s.

In Europe, the administration showed affinity for West Germany's conservative, anti-communist government led by Konrad Adenauer, who adamantly opposed any negotiations with the Soviets on Germany which might involve compromises in the Western position. Determined that West Germany be rearmed, Dulles pressured the anxious French to choose between participation by German soldiers in a common European army or German membership in NATO. The French Assembly reluctantly approved the latter on December 24, 1954, and West Germany joined NATO the following year. With West Germany in

NATO, and with Moscow responding by creating a formal military alliance of its own in 1955, the Warsaw Treaty Organization, the military division of Europe was now complete.

In Asia, Dulles and some other high officials in the spring of 1954 flirted with the idea of using atomic bombs against Ho Chi Minh's forces in order to forestall a communist victory in Indochina, but Eisenhower and congressional leaders demurred. At a news conference on April 6, the president, citing the strategic and economic importance of Southeast Asia, did endorse the so-called "domino theory," the view that the fall of one nation in a region to communism would lead to rapid communist victories in the others, and he also let Dulles travel to London to try to persuade Prime Minister Churchill of the necessity of intervention to save the French. Churchill and his foreign minister, Anthony Eden, remained unpersuaded, and on May 7 the beleaguered French garrison at Dien Bien Phu surrendered.

When the Geneva Conference that summer awarded Ho Chi Minh only the northern half of Vietnam, pending unifying elections in 1956, Dulles was angry that the communist-led independence movement had won anything. Pledging generous public aid and private CIA assistance, the United States quickly helped to establish the strongly anti-communist Ngo Dinh Diem as the new ruler in the southern half of Vietnam, and supported him in his refusal to cooperate in holding the elections in 1956. The United States also worked to disrupt the Hanoi government by urging Catholics to leave and by sponsoring secret raids from South Vietnam and Taiwan. In Iran, in Guatemala, and now in South Vietnam, American money and power seemed nearly invincible.

The new Soviet leaders respected America's economic and military might, and they also wanted a better relationship with the United States than had existed during Stalin's last years. During the spring and summer of 1953 the new premier, Georgi Malenkov, repeatedly called for improved relations with the West; the Soviet press published much less anti-American propaganda, and *Pravda* even published the full text of

Eisenhower's speech of April 16 calling for settlement of outstanding disputes and steps toward disarmament. The Soviets were helpful in concluding the armistice in Korea in July, and they renewed Stalin's intriguing offer of 1952 to negotiate a reunified, neutral Germany. Sensing the improved atmosphere, Churchill on May 11 called for a summit conference of world leaders, but American officials, notably Dulles, were cool to the idea. The American ambassador in Moscow, Charles Bohlen, later regreted that he did not urge Eisenhower to accept the proposal for a summit in 1953, for "there might have been opportunities for an adjustment of some of the outstanding questions, particularly regarding Germany." The cautious, anti-communist president developed a "stock answer" to questions from reporters about a possible summit meeting: "I would not go to a Summit because of friendly words and plausible promises by the men of the Kremlin; actual deeds giving some indication of a Communist readiness to negotiate constructively will have to be produced before I would agree to such a meeting."

Could there have been substantial progress in resolving such key East-West issues as Germany and arms control in 1953 or 1954? One cannot be sure, for Churchill's proposal to start serious negotiations quickly was not implemented. But there clearly would have been enormously difficult obstacles to overcome. Dulles and other State Department analysts, with their Cold War mind-set, were refusing to believe that any significant changes had taken place in the Soviet approach to world affairs. Many Americans, having been sold on the unmitigated evil of communism and on the necessity of sacrifices to wage the Cold War, would have been quite reluctant to support a sudden shift in policy, especially with McCarthy still claiming that conciliatory leaders were traitors. Allied leaders like Adenauer also would have opposed a sudden shift in U.S. policy. The Soviets, for their part, were involved in 1953 and 1954 in a serious struggle for power in the Kremlin that was hardly conducive to effective negotiations. They also were involved in 1953 in putting down a revolt in East Germany and in developing an operational hydrogen bomb, neither of which improved relations with the

West. In short, domestic constraints and the burdens of alliance systems would have made it hard for either side to have made the large concessions necessary for a substantial shift toward détente. Nevertheless, one can fault American leaders for not exploring more fully the possibility of mutually acceptable agreements with Russia before additional alliance-building virtually froze the situation in Germany by the mid-1950s.

The conditions necessary for top-level Soviet-American talks finally existed in 1955. With Khrushchev having emerged as the chief Soviet leader and negotiator, with Dulles having achieved his goal of West German participation in NATO, and with Russia showing "constructiveness" by negotiating with the West a peace treaty for Austria in the spring of 1955, the stage was set for the summit meeting in Geneva that July, the first such meeting since Potsdam exactly a decade before. The Russians were represented by Premier Nikolai Bulganin and by Communist party leader Khrushchev, who held the real power; the Americans, by Eisenhower and Dulles, who had urged the president not to go but who at least was there to insure that the president did not give anything away. British and French leaders also were present, but obviously in a secondary capacity. Eisenhower had "no illusions" about the summit's likelihood of success, and he and Dulles assured congressmen that "Geneva was not going to be another Yalta." Khrushchev, who had little experience in international affairs, remembered being worried about whether the Soviet leaders could "represent our country competently" and "keep the other side from intimidating us." Thus, neither leader was expecting that the conference would accomplish very much.

Not surprisingly, their modest expectations were fulfilled. Taking place in an atmosphere more conducive to press coverage and posturing than to serious negotiations, the leaders' statements repeatedly exposed the gulf separating the two sides. Each side professed to desire the unification of Germany, but only on its own terms. The British and Russians traded proposals for demilitarizing Central Europe, each unacceptable to the other. To counter Soviet disarmament proposals made earlier in the

THE INSTITUTIONALIZED COLD WAR 69

year, Eisenhower dramatically announced an "open skies" proposal in which the Americans and Soviets would exchange maps
of their military installations and permit aerial inspection in
order to lessen fear of secret military buildups and the possibility
of surprise attacks. The Soviets, who traditionally feared es-
pionage and sought to conceal their actual military weakness,
naturally rejected this proposal. "We knew the Soviets wouldn't
accept it," Eisenhower admitted later. As at Potsdam, the major
specific agreement at Geneva was to refer all areas of discord to
subsequent meetings of the Council of Foreign Ministers.

Despite the predictable disagreement on major issues, the
Geneva summit was valuable because it introduced the leaders of
the two sides to each other. Eisenhower and Khrushchev knew
very little about each other prior to Geneva; the president, for
example, did not realize until well into the conference that
Khrushchev was "the real boss" in the Soviet delegation. Informal social gatherings often proved more useful in breaking
down barriers than the formal meetings in which leaders tended
to read from prepared texts. Once at dinner Eisenhower expressed his concern that hydrogen bombs could "easily and un-
wittingly destroy the entire Northern Hemisphere." "War has
failed," he told the Soviets with his usual unaffected sincerity.
"The only way to save the world is through diplomacy." His listeners nodded vigorously in approval. Khrushchev had included
General Georgi Zhukov in the Soviet delegation because he
hoped that Zhukov's friendship with Eisenhower during World
War II might "serve as the basis for conversations that would
lead to an easing of tension between our countries." But,
Khrushchev noted colorfully in his memoirs, "that vicious cur
Dulles was always prowling around Eisenhower, snapping at
him if he got out of line."

More than anything else, the Geneva summit proved to the
world that the leaders of the Soviet Union and the West could sit
down and discuss the issues that divided them, and then shake
hands and issue a civilized communiqué at the end of the meetings. The summit thus dealt a serious blow to the assumption,
common in both countries in earlier years, that all-out war be-

tween the two sides was inevitable. As Eisenhower noted in his memoirs:

> . . . in spite of what happened thereafter, the cordial atmosphere of the talks, dubbed the "Spirit of Geneva," never faded entirely. Indeed, the way was opened for some increase in intercourse between East and West—there began, between the United States and Russia, exchanges of trade exhibitions, scientists, musicians, and other performers; visits were made by Mikoyan and Kozlov to the United States, and returned, by Vice President Nixon and my brother Milton, to the Soviet Union and Poland. These were small beginnings, but they could not have transpired in the atmosphere prevailing before Geneva.

Cultural, economic, and scientific exchanges between the Soviet Union and the United States, moribund since the late 1940s, were renewed in 1955 and continued to expand on a fairly regular basis during the next two decades. Soviet pianist Emil Gilels and violinist David Oistrakh made a big hit with American audiences in the fall of 1955, and a largely black American company performing the musical *Porgy and Bess* proved a tremendous attraction in Moscow and Leningrad that winter. After additional successful exchanges on an ad hoc basis, the United States and Russia signed a formal exchange agreement on January 28, 1958.

Bob Loftus, an American who was involved in arranging a tour for forty Russian home builders in the United States in 1955 and who went to Russia on a tour of American home builders in 1956, recalled that one of the Russians told him before leaving this country, "We just don't believe that people who are spending so much wealth on their homes and their families are preparing for war against my country, as we have been told so many times." When Loftus was attending a performance in the Kiev Opera House the next year, the man's teenage daughter whispered in his ear: "You must live in a wonderful country. My father has told us all about it."

Although cultural exchanges obviously have not always been this successful, one should never underestimate the importance of nonofficial contacts in improving the general atmosphere in which Soviet-American relations have been conducted since 1955. They often have been especially meaningful to Russians, who generally have had far fewer opportunities than Americans for travel and for contact with the outside world. Equally significant to Russians concerned that Westerners view them as inferior, the exchanges have symbolized a spirit of equality between their country and the United States. While the exchanges and the eventual development of Soviet-American trade certainly have not guaranteed good relations, they have served as something of a safety net to inhibit a drop in Soviet-American relations to the level of 1950–1952. Exchanges of all types may be viewed, therefore, as a concrete, enduring manifestation of the "spirit of Geneva."

The Second Dangerous Phase, 1956–1962

Soviet-American relations during the late 1950s and early 1960s seem to support the maxim (reaffirmed in the late 1970s) that if relationships between the two superpowers do not continue to improve, they decline; in other words, superpower relationships do not remain fairly stable, as they frequently do between a great power and a lesser one. While improved official and informal relationships increase the chances for constructive bilateral communication, this period demonstrates that they do not in themselves overcome long-standing patterns of conflicting interests and mutual distrust. To prevent the worsening of relations, positive breakthroughs need to occur on at least one key issue, in this case perhaps Berlin or nuclear testing. The failure of both sides to reverse the downward slide in Soviet-American relations in the late 1950s thus contributed to the frenzied, warlike atmosphere of the early 1960s.

Zbigniew Brzezinski has called the period of the late 1950s and early 1960s in East-West relations a time of "premature Soviet globalism." "Soviet international activity acquired for the first time a distinctly global range," Brzezinski observed.

But such globalism was premature, he argued, because Russia did not yet have the military or economic power to sustain far-flung interests. Under pressure domestically and from within his bloc to make tangible progress on East-West issues, especially Berlin, Khrushchev exaggerated Soviet strength and threatened the West in the hope that his diplomatic initiatives could succeed. Not surprisingly, his apparent animosity—combined with rhetorical and material support for "wars of national liberation" in developing nations—triggered the hostility and uncompromising resolve in the West which the events of 1953–1955 had only slightly moderated.

It would be inaccurate to blame Soviet actions alone for the tensions that culminated in the Cuban missile crisis of 1962. For if Russia was pursuing a somewhat unpredictable policy of premature globalism, the United States was embarked on a full-fledged policy of mature globalism, involving the nation's determination, in President Kennedy's famous words, "that we shall pay any price, bear any burden, meet any hardship, support any friend, oppose any foe to assure the survival and the success of liberty." A 1978 Brookings Institution study of American armed intervention abroad between 1946 and 1975 confirmed the historical accuracy of Kennedy's vow: military interventions short of war peaked in the late 1950s and early 1960s, with an average of twelve incidents occurring each year between 1956 and 1965. If extensive covert activities, military and economic aid packages, and other types of official and nonofficial actions directed against "communism" are added in, there can be little doubt that America's Cold War interventionism was reaching its peak.

While U.S. interventionism of the 1950s and 1960s sometimes had tragic consequences, it must be noted that this was not always the case, and that, moreover, American officials often were idealistic in assisting in "nation-building" in the Third World. "The key point is that this massive U.S. intervention, both overt and covert, was aimed politically at building what our people thought of as more just and progressive societies," Wallace Irwin, Jr., a former U.S. official, recalled. "We weren't just against the Reds; we were for democracy and we believed ourselves to have a missionary duty to export it."

Using both pressure and persuasion, American officials sometimes lessened corruption in developing nations, and insisted successfully that elections be held and reforms be carried out. In short, while military interventions like the Bay of Pigs in Cuba and Vietnam are justly remembered, the efforts of numerous officials and private groups to improve conditions in the Third World—while simultaneously combatting communism—should not be forgotten.

The year 1956 was a difficult one in world affairs for both Russia and the United States. In a passionate, secret, four-hour speech to the Twentieth Party Congress on February 24, Khrushchev denounced Stalin for domestic crimes and mistakes in foreign policy, endorsed "peaceful coexistence" and steps to end the arms race, and indicated that the Kremlin would relax its tight control in the Soviet Union and recognize diversity in the international Communist movement. The CIA quickly obtained copies of the speech, made it public in the West, and distributed it throughout Eastern Europe.

Partly due to the speech and partly due to the long buildup of pressures for de-Stalinization in Eastern Europe, demands for change spread rapidly. By summer Poland—strategically crucial as the main buffer state between Russia and Germany—was in turmoil, and the Soviets faced a serious challenge to their authority there. The Polish Communist party was split between old-line Stalinists, who wanted to use force to repress the demands for change, and those who demanded greater independence from Moscow and believed that concessions needed to be made in order to win greater popular support. Wishing to avoid military intervention, the Soviets in October finally agreed that a communist leader associated with the second viewpoint, Wladyslaw Gomulka, would be permitted to take power. "There is more than one road to socialism," an exultant Gomulka declared on October 20. He warned the Kremlin that the Polish people would "defend themselves with all means;

they will not be pushed off the road of democratization." Although Poland continued to be communist and remained in the Russian bloc, these developments weakened Soviet influence there and set an example which other satellite nations emulated.

Events in Hungary in the fall of 1956 were more tragic. Emboldened by the successful defiance of Soviet rule in Warsaw, students took to the streets in Budapest on October 23 to demand that Imre Nagy replace the unpopular Stalinist rulers. As the turmoil spread, the Soviets agreed to the change, and by October 28 they even agreed to remove their tanks from around Budapest. Responding to the demands of students and workers, Nagy announced that Hungary planned to leave the Warsaw Pact and permit the creation of opposition parties.

To the Soviets, the "counterrevolution" in Hungary was going much too far. After winning the support of Gomulka and other East European leaders, Khrushchev ordered Soviet forces to crush the rebellion. The poorly armed students and workers fighting Soviet tanks on the streets of Budapest in early November won tremendous sympathy in the West, but the Russians quickly restored order, executed Nagy, and imposed a regime much harsher than Gomulka's or Tito's. American newspapers thus had fresh material for their favorite ongoing story, the horrors of communism, while the Russian press emphasized their nation's vigilance in guarding the Eastern bloc against Western imperialism. The Russian press did not explain why the revolt in Hungary had taken place, and the American press generally was not interested in Russia's reasons for suppressing it. The communications gap between the two sides, a basic feature of the Cold War, continued to flourish.

While the Eastern bloc in 1956 was dealing with pressures for de-Stalinization and freedom from Soviet rule, the Western alliance was feeling the strains of de-colonization and defiance of American leadership. In late October, only days before the Soviets moved on Budapest, Israel, France, and Great Britain launched coordinated attacks against Egypt, a former British protectorate. The Anglo-French aim was to repossess the Suez Canal and, apparently, to overthrow Egyptian President Gamal

Abdel Nasser. Furious that he had not been informed in advance and disapproving of an action reminiscent of nineteenth-century colonialism, Eisenhower went on television and announced that the United States could not accept "one code of international conduct for those who oppose us and another for our friends."

Fearing increased Russian influence in the Middle East, the administration took strong and successful diplomatic action at the United Nations and elsewhere to force the removal of the foreign forces from Egypt. Meanwhile the Soviets made strong threats against Britain and France, and even proposed to Eisenhower that America and Russia conduct a joint military intervention to restore peace in the Middle East. Faced with hostile world opinion and pressure from the two superpowers, Britain and France halted their attack and removed their troops by December, and Israel, under intense American pressure, followed suit by the following March.

Despite their understandable anger at the time of the Suez crisis, American officials bore considerable responsibility for precipitating it. Nasser, whose neutralism in the East-West struggle angered Dulles, had made a deal in September 1955 with the Russians to exchange Egyptian cotton for Czechoslovakian weapons. Anxious to limit Soviet influence, Dulles had promised that December to help Egypt build a large dam at Aswan on the upper Nile to provide electricity and water for irrigation. When Dulles, angered at the Czech arms deal, reneged on this pledge in July 1956, Nasser nationalized the Suez Canal, removing it from British control. Infuriated by the seizure and tired of following Dulles's overbearing advice (in this case, not to use force against Egypt), the British, French, and Israelis finally had decided to strike. The inept American hand in the whole affair left some bitterness among officials in London and Paris, bitterness that harmed NATO and which still rankled when the United States asked for help in Vietnam a decade later.

Finally, the Suez crisis damaged Soviet-American relations, despite their common opposition to the attack. Wishing to minimize the harm to the Western alliance and to maintain America's special relationship with Israel, Eisenhower in his public

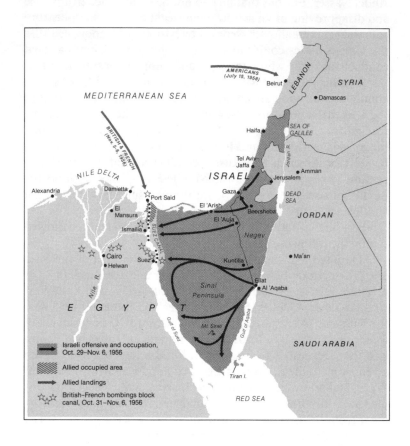

AMERICANS
(July 15, 1958)

Beirut •   LEBANON   SYRIA

MEDITERRANEAN SEA

• Damascus

BRITISH & FRENCH
(Nov. 5-6, 1956)

Haifa •   SEA OF
GALILEE

NILE DELTA

Tel Aviv •
Jaffa

ISRAEL

• Amman

Jerusalem •

Alexandria •

Damietta •

☆ Port Said

Gaza •

DEAD
SEA

El 'Arish •

• El
Mansura

El 'Auja •

Beersheba •

JORDAN

Ismailia •

Negev

☆ ☆
☆

• Cairo
• Helwan

Nile R.

Suez ☆

Kuntilla •

• Ma'an

Eilat •
• Al 'Aqaba

E   G   Y   P   T

Sinai
Peninsula

Gulf of Suez

Mt. Sinai

Gulf of Aqaba

SAUDI ARABIA

➤ Israeli offensive and occupation,
Oct. 29–Nov. 6, 1956

Allied occupied area

➤ Allied landings

☆☆☆ British–French bombings block
canal, Oct. 31–Nov. 6, 1956

Tiran I.

RED SEA

statements repeatedly made it appear that Russia was the real
culprit in the Middle East. And the Soviets, in their public statements and diplomatic notes, engaged in denunciations, threats,
and appeals to international morality wholly inconsistent with
their own actions at that very moment in Hungary. When
Khrushchev in early November threatened a nuclear attack on
England and France if they refused to leave Egypt, Eisenhower
placed the Strategic Air Command on full alert and told an aide

that he was ready, if Western Europe was attacked, to hit Russia "with *everything* in the bucket." Such threats and counter-threats, backed by unprecedented nuclear capabilities on both sides, were not uncommon during this second dangerous phase of the Cold War.

Throughout 1955 and 1956 a strong plurality of Gallup's respondents had viewed the Republicans as the party "best able to maintain peace." In February 1956, for example, 36 percent chose the Republicans while only 18 percent selected the Democrats; the remainder were either undecided or believed that the two parties were equally competent in this area. Many election analysts considered Eisenhower's success in keeping the nation at peace an important factor in his lead over Democratic candidate Adlai Stevenson going into the final weeks of the 1956 campaign; and, in their view, the crises in Hungary and Egypt turned a comfortable victory into a landslide, as many undecided voters concluded that they should support the experienced president in a time of crisis. In May 1957, after the two crises had ended, Republicans led Democrats on this question by an impressive 45 to 19 percent. And yet by July 1960 Democrats led Republicans 41 to 25 percent on the question of the party best able to "increase respect" for America in the world.

What had happened to erode the Republicans' position and, in effect, to make a Democratic victory in 1960 more likely? The answer, of course, is plenty, more than could be discussed in detail here. There were, as mentioned earlier, tensions with mainland China in the Taiwan straits region, and difficulties in such places as Lebanon, Laos, Berlin, Cuba, and the Congo (now Zaire). A nation with global responsibilities had to accept wide-ranging difficulties and expenses, spokesmen for the State Department and the so-called foreign policy establishment in New York kept reminding the public. But more than anything else, the tensions of these years that gradually eroded the Republican position resulted from frightening advances in military technology and in potential military capabilities. Incorrect without necessarily being insincere, Democrats, disgruntled military officers, and journalists could use these developments to claim that the United States was falling dangerously behind Russia in the arms race and to call for massive new defense expenditures.

When Eisenhower rejected these demands as unnecessary for the nation's defense and potentially harmful to its economy, the more hard-line Democrats, such as Senators Stuart Symington of Missouri and Henry Jackson of Washington, could suggest that the president was flirting with disaster. "Though by early 1959 we knew the Soviet Union still led us in certain areas of missile research and production . . . ," Eisenhower noted in his memoirs, "we also knew that our total defense capabilities—including manned bombers, emerging long-range ballistic missiles, and nuclear weapons of all kinds—had a superiority overwhelming enough to deter the Soviet leaders from aggression." Fearing Russia and lacking the knowledge to evaluate complex defense issues, the general public, as in the late 1940s and again in the late 1970s, tended to be susceptible to warnings about America's "weakness."

The public's susceptibility to "missile gap" charges began on October 4, 1957, when Russia stunned Western opinion by launching the first man-made satellite, *Sputnik I.* Russia might have a larger army, Europeans and Americans had believed; but surely the United States, which had first developed atomic weapons and numerous other scientific marvels, was years ahead in technology. Not necessarily, the Russians demonstrated in one stroke, and Khrushchev predictably boasted about it. A summary of *Sputnik's* implications—more useful in illustrating the widely-shared perception that America now was on the defensive than in explaining what actually had happened—appeared shortly thereafter in the *New York Times:*

Militarily, the launching of *Sputnik* means that Russia is ahead of the U.S. in rocket development. That lends substance to the Soviet claim of having at least a prototype of the "ultimate weapon"—the intercontinental ballistic missile.

Politically, the satellite gave the Russians an opportunity to proclaim the Soviet Union a first-class power whose views must carry weight in every capital. . . . They are already moving to undermine

Western alliances by suggesting that the U.S. and Russia deal directly with each other on such questions as control of arms and spheres of influence . . .

Psychologically, Moscow used the satellite as ground for assertions of scientific preeminence and military power, as proof that communism is the wave of the future. The impact of those assertions on other nations, particularly the uncommitted, could be formidable.

American analysts understandably assumed that the Soviets would press their temporary advantage in high-powered rocket boosters and quickly develop a large ICBM force capable of raining nuclear weapons on American cities. Instead, the Soviets decided to deploy only a few of the expensive liquid-fuel missiles in the next few years, thus waiting until cheaper solid-fuel missiles became feasible in the mid-1960s. But this decision to show restraint in the arms race—and thus to remain much more vulnerable to American nuclear attack than the United States was to Soviet attack—was not matched by diplomatic restraint on Khrushchev's part. Under pressure from the Chinese to show toughness in dealing with the "imperialists" and from East Germany to resolve the Berlin issue, Khrushchev embarked in 1958 on a series of gambling, dramatic initiatives designed to break the East-West stalemate and to achieve tangible gains for Russia.

Khrushchev's difficulties in regard to Berlin—especially the relative affluence of West Berlin and the departure since 1949 of approximately three million East Germans through West Berlin to the greater freedom and opportunity of West Germany—caused serious strains for Walter Ulbricht's communist government. From the Soviet viewpoint, the situation was at least as bad as it had been when Stalin had tried to force a resolution of the issue a decade before. Unless Khrushchev could convince or coerce the West to be willing to stabilize the situation through such steps as establishing diplomatic relations with Ulbricht's regime, the situation for the Soviets apparently could only get worse. But West German politicians of all major parties agreed during these years that formal recognition of East Germany—in effect, abandoning forever the dream of German reunification "in freedom"—was politically unthinkable; and Washington gave its unqualified backing to this West German position.

Having failed at Geneva and elsewhere to convince Western leaders to negotiate to ease Russia's problems in Germany, Khrushchev in 1958 began to try to coerce them to do so. On November 10 he announced that the West would have six months in which to negotiate with the Soviets concerning its rights in Berlin. If serious negotiations had not begun by then, he warned that Russia would sign a separate peace treaty with East Germany, and that thereafter the West would have to deal directly with Ulbricht's government. Responding to this diplomacy by ultimatum, hawks in Congress urged a sharp buildup in American military strength, but Eisenhower refused, commenting after one National Security Council meeting that "in this gamble, we are not going to be betting white chips, building up the pot gradually and fearfully. Khrushchev should know that when we decide to act, our whole stack will be in the pot."

If Eisenhower did not increase defense expenditures, neither did he negotiate under duress. Instead, he calmly denied that a crisis existed. Asked by a reporter in March 1959 whether he would "use nuclear war . . . to defend free Berlin," the president replied: "Well, I don't know how you could free anything with nuclear weapons." Characteristically, Khrushchev alternated between making conciliatory statements and threatening West European leaders with nuclear destruction if they refused to negotiate. But he let the deadline pass without signing the treaty with East Germany, and he accepted Eisenhower's invitation to visit the United States in September 1959.

Khrushchev's thirteen-day visit—the first ever by a top Soviet leader—was one vast media event. As the stocky, outspoken premier visited Washington, New York, cities and rural areas in the West and Midwest, and finally returned to Washington for talks at nearby Camp David, the press and television followed his every word and action. When Secretary of the Treasury Douglas Dillon asked him a hostile question about the meaning of peaceful coexistence, Khrushchev responded, "Mr. Dillon, if you don't understand what peaceful coexistence between two systems is, I'm sorry. The time will come when you'll have to learn." In New York he responded to a group of businessmen extolling capitalism with the comment, "Every duck praises its marsh." After seeing a dance routine in Hollywood, he remarked that "humanity's face is more beautiful than its backside." According to a Gallup poll at the time, 52 percent considered Khrushchev's visit a "good thing," 19 percent thought it was a "bad thing," and 29 percent were neutral or undecided.

In his cordial meetings with Eisenhower at Camp David, Khrushchev agreed to abandon his ultimatum on Berlin if the president would attend another summit conference the following spring. In addition to Berlin, the two leaders spent considerable time discussing Eisenhower's greatest concern of his last years in office, the need to end the arms race. "You know, we really should come to some sort of an agreement in order to stop this fruitless, really wasteful rivalry," Eisenhower commented. "That's one of our dreams . . . ," Khrushchev responded. "But how can we agree? On what basis?" Although no major arms control agreements were reached before Eisenhower left office, it is significant that the ultimately successful test ban negotiations began in Geneva in 1958, and that both sides observed a moratorium on atmospheric testing for nearly three years until the international climate worsened in 1961.

The hopes of Khrushchev and Eisenhower to substantially improve relations between their two countries, already strained by criticisms of coexistence by China and reluctance by France and West Germany to move too fast, came crashing to earth in May 1960. As with *Sputnik* 2 1/2 years before, military technology played a major role. Since 1956 the CIA, under the president's direction, had been using a high-flying, lightweight U-2 aircraft to conduct surveillance of Soviet military installations. The Soviets knew about these flights and, Khrushchev recalled, "were more infuriated and disgusted every time a violation [of Soviet air space] occurred." To the Soviets, the flights were not only an insult to their sovereignty, but also a painful reminder of Soviet inferiority to the West in most areas of military technology. The Russian leaders thus were elated when, after apparently being hit by a Soviet antiaircraft missile, a U-2 crashed to the ground in central Russia on May 1 and its pilot, Francis Gary Powers, who had bailed out, was captured.

The ensuing events offer a classic illustration of the triumph of national pride over conciliation in a time of unexpected tension. The administration first tried the cover story that a weather plane might have strayed accidentally over Soviet territory. Then, when Khrushchev produced Powers, the wrecked plane, and details of the U-2's mission, Eisenhower finally admitted the overflight. Wishing to maintain reasonably good relations between the two countries, Khrushchev carefully avoided blaming the president. But Eisenhower took full responsibility for the flight and, while saying that the U-2 missions would now stop, refused to apologize for Powers's flight. It had been necessary, he maintained, because of Russia's military secrecy. Although the administration mishandled the U-2 incident, it must be noted in fairness that the flights had provided the intelligence information that had enabled Eisenhower to resist the demands for higher defense expenditures.

Now it was Khrushchev's turn to defend his nation's pride. At the four-power summit meeting in Paris on May 16, the Soviet premier, in a bitter speech, accused the United States of aggression, demanded an apology for the U-2 as a condition for continuing the meetings, and withdrew his invitation to Eisenhower to visit Russia. When Eisenhower in a calm response refused to meet Khrushchev's demands, the Soviet delegation walked out, thus ending the summit before any substantive discussions had taken place. Because of the reactions on both sides to the U-2 incident, therefore, the president's sincere effort to improve Soviet-American relations collapsed eight months before he left office.

In his memoirs Khrushchev claimed credit for helping Senator Kennedy defeat Vice-President Nixon in the election that fall. Wishing to help Kennedy, Soviet leaders made the decision, Khrushchev revealed, to turn down the administration's request to release Powers before the election. Moreover, if the summit had been successful and if Eisenhower had visited Russia, the Republicans could have stood in 1960 as the party which had lessened East-West tensions. Instead, due to the heightened Cold War tensions which continued throughout the year, Kennedy was able to keep Nixon on the defensive on foreign affairs in the campaign, insisting repeatedly that Eisenhower and Nixon had not done enough to defeat international communism. Although the election of 1960 is remembered primarily for its series of debates between the two relatively youthful and skilled compaigners, it might equally be remembered as a high water mark of harsh Cold War rhetoric by both parties.

Whether Khrushchev's hostility to the West in 1960 actually helped Kennedy is not clear, for the young senator won by the thinnest of margins at a time when there were far more registered Democrats than Republicans. What is apparent in retrospect is that Khrushchev's hard-line approach affected the new administration's policy toward Russia, and that he ultimately had the most to lose from the continuing deterioration of Soviet-American relations after May 1960.

As during Eisenhower's last years, Cold War issues dominated public discourse during Kennedy's first two. In addition to unresolved problems relating to Berlin and to the frightening technology of the arms race, the Democratic administration which took office in January 1961 faced immediate competition with Russia in the Congo, Laos, and Cuba. It also faced a Republican party which, shorn of the calming leadership of Eisenhower, demanded that Kennedy take an uncompromising stand toward international communism.

As there had been partisan pressure to take a stronger stand on China and Russia during the first dangerous phase of the Cold War, so there was heavy partisan pressure to take a bellicose position on Cuba and other Cold War issues in the early 1960s. On Cuba, for example, leading Democrats denounced the incumbent Republicans during 1960 for "doing nothing" about Premier Fidel Castro, and leading Republicans leveled precisely the same charge against the incumbent Democrats in 1961 and 1962. The result was a political atmosphere within the United States which was in some ways even more hard-line toward any evidence of communist activity abroad than it had been a decade before.

During his first two months in office, Kennedy gave more personal attention to the situation in Laos than to any other single issue. American policy in the late 1950s in this small, land-locked nation in Southeast Asia had contributed substantially to the problems which Kennedy now faced. Fearing the involvement of local communists in the government, the Eisenhower administration in 1959 had helped to overthrow the neutralist government of Souvanna Phouma and install a pro-Western one. But this new government had proved much less viable than the previous one, thus allowing the communist Pathet Lao to gain both support and additional territory. Moreover, shortly after Kennedy took office the Soviets airlifted military supplies to the Pathet Lao.

Applying the usual Cold War double standard, American officials professed to be horrified by this evidence of Soviet activity in Laos, a country in which the CIA had been doing most of the supplying of arms and manipulating of officials. Accordingly, Kennedy went on television on March 15 to warn the Russians that the United States might go to war in Laos if the pro-Western government's position continued to deteriorate. Neither Kennedy nor Khrushchev wanted war in this obscure nation, however, and negotiations to neutralize Laos began later that spring.

American officials estimated that, in the absence of direct American military intervention, the communists gradually would take control in Laos. In order to forestall a similar fate in neighboring South Vietnam, the administration moved in the spring and summer of 1961 to increase military aid to Diem's government and, beginning in early 1962, to send several thousand military "advisers" as well. It is probably helpful to Eisenhower's historical reputation that he left office when he did, for the time bomb that his administration had planted in South Vietnam was getting ready to explode by the early 1960s. Diem's autocratic government was becoming increasingly unpopular, as large public demonstrations and repeated self-immolations by Buddhist monks in 1963 confirmed. Diem's unpopularity, in turn, played into the hands of Viet Cong guerrillas, who began in 1960 to operate openly, with support from North Vietnam, and succeeded in building a strong infrastructure in rural areas. Fearing sharp criticism from conservatives if he "lost" South Vietnam the way Truman had "lost" China, Kennedy gradually increased American military personnel in South Vietnam to 16,500 while at the same time urging Diem to make reforms designed to win popular support. Although generally wishing to avoid publicity about the war in Vietnam, the administration did not seek to hide the fact that its new emphasis in military training on counterinsurgency (a fancy name for antiguerrilla warfare) was being tested there. Also being tested—and found wanting—in both the Eisenhower and the Kennedy-Johnson years was the theory of "nation-building," which was carried out increasingly behind barbed wire in "strategic hamlets." In addition to difficulties inherent in applying American ideas to Vietnamese circumstances, this program failed because of relentless Viet Cong attacks and because of the South Vietnamese government's half-hearted effort to implement it.

Except for occasional questioning of policy toward Diem in liberal magazines, there was little domestic criticism of Kennedy's approach until the summer of 1963. Even then the criticism was directed mainly against American support of Diem, not against the Cold War premises underlying the U.S. military involvement. When Diem was overthrown with American approval on November 1, 1963, leading officials and journalists welcomed the development as strengthening the U.S. position in Southeast Asia. And when Kennedy was assassinated in Dallas three weeks later, the new president, Lyndon Johnson, and other top U.S. officials believed that America's prestige and honor were at stake in the continuing war in Vietnam. Like a slowly developing but incurable cancer, the commitment there was becoming more malignant with each passing administration.

In 1961 and 1962, Cuba was an incomparably larger public issue than either Laos or Vietnam. It was a hundred times closer to American soil (roughly ninety miles versus nine thousand), it traditionally had been within the American sphere of influence, it had a leader whom the American news media tended to picture as a devil, it had exiles who settled in the United States and stirred popular opinion against Castro, and it had much more public support from Khrushchev than did the Pathet Lao or the Viet Cong. When Castro had come to power in January 1959, many Americans had welcomed the change from the brutal, unpopular Batista regime. But relations between Cuba and the nation many Latin Americans had long considered the "colossus of the North" declined gradually in 1959 and more rapidly after Russia signed a trade agreement with Cuba the following February and Castro announced that his sympathies were with the socialist camp. Before the revolution, American interests had owned well over half of several key sectors of the Cuban economy; what American officials overlooked in their rush to denounce Castro's policies was that it would have been virtually impossible for Castro to implement significant social change in Cuba while fully compensating American economic interests there.

By the time Kennedy took office, the CIA had developed a specific plan to train Cuban exiles to invade the island and precipitate the overthrow of Castro's government. Kennedy had insisted during the campaign that the government should be doing more to topple Castro, and now he could turn his words into actions. Although somewhat skeptical, Kennedy approved the continuation of planning for the mission and, in early April, approved the invasion itself. But he put the CIA on notice that American involvement would remain limited, that he was making no promises to have American troops bail out the fourteen hundred exiles if they encountered difficulties. Unfortunately, CIA operatives failed to explain fully to the exiles the limited nature of the U.S. commitment, thus contributing to the bitterness within the exile community when the operation quickly failed and most of the invaders were killed or captured. Widely criticized by world leaders and by common citizens in Latin America, Western Europe, and elsewhere, the Bay of Pigs invasion remains a prime example of superpower arrogance and foolishness in a period of high international tensions.

Khrushchev soon demonstrated that he could be as foolhardy in his own way as Kennedy had been in his. At a summit meeting with the president at Vienna in early June, the Soviet leader was as blunt and blustering to Kennedy as he had been to Eisenhower the year before. Although Khrushchev did agree to help find a peaceful solution in Laos, he insisted that Russia retained the right to aid liberation struggles in the Third World. More ominously, he reimposed his deadline on resolving the German issue, and declared that Berlin must become a "free city" without Allied military forces. This time, Khrushchev insisted, he was not bluffing: the decision to sign a separate treaty with East Germany if the deadline passed was irrevocable. "What I said might have sounded like a threat to Kennedy," Khrushchev admitted later.

Upon his return to Washington, Kennedy gave a somber televised report to the nation on his trip, but declined to mention the ultimatum. Khrushchev, who was under tremendous pressure from East Germany and from his Kremlin colleagues to finally resolve the Berlin issue, publicized his threat on Berlin in mid-June.

Like Eisenhower during the preceding Berlin crisis, Kennedy soon was subjected to demands from hard liners within the government, from the opposition party in Congress, and from much of the press to take firm measures to demonstrate Western resolve. Unlike his experienced predecessor, the new president acceded to these demands, and in a television address on July 25 he asked Congress for $3.2 billion to supplement the regular defense budget, for authority to call up the reserves, and for a stepped-up civil defense program. As was its practice during the

Cold War, Congress moved quickly to approve all the military measures Kennedy requested. Leaving no doubt of his "toughness," the president soon called up the reserves for a one-year tour of duty and sponsored programs urging the public to build fallout shelters for use in the event of nuclear war with Russia. Dismayed that the United States was proceeding with a rapid arms buildup at a time when it already had substantial nuclear superiority, Khrushchev insisted that the West was overreacting to his demands.

Fortunately for East-West relations if not for the residents of Berlin, Khrushchev and Ulbricht found their own way of stopping the hemorrhage of East Germans to the West, and thus of making the presence of free West Berlin in their midst more tolerable for the East German government. In the early morning of August 13, East German security forces began sealing off all roads between East Berlin and West Berlin, and within days a heavily guarded concrete-block wall separated the two halves of the city. The Western powers protested this move, but, again recognizing the post–World War II division of Europe, did nothing effective to counter it. Like the crushing of the Hungarian rebellion, the building of the Berlin Wall provided the West with valuable propaganda, for who would want to live in a country that refuses to let its disaffected citizens leave?

Although Westerners denounced this Russian move at the time, it actually helped to defuse the Berlin crisis of 1961 and, by stabilizing the situation within East Germany, paved the way for the subsequent easing of tensions in the area. But these consequences are much easier to grasp in retrospect than they were at the time, for American officials had to continue to deal through 1962 with persistent Soviet harassment of Western troop transports and military aircraft coming into Berlin. Khrushchev again let his deadline for the peace treaty with East Germany pass, but he was determined to keep reminding the Western powers that the situation in Berlin would remain abnormal until they established working relationships with the Ulbricht regime. So powerful was Berlin as a symbol of Cold War tensions that, while the administration feverishly prepared its response in the Cuban missile crisis the next fall, many reporters assumed that the crisis atmosphere apparent in Washington probably involved Berlin.

In discussing the earlier dangerous phase of the Cold War, I emphasized the breakdown of effective communications between the two sides and the tendency to view the other side's actions in the worst possible light. Although there was much more diplomatic contact during the second dangerous phase, the same trends were apparent. Whether the immediate issue was Laos, Berlin, nuclear testing, or whatever, those in Washington and Moscow with a fervent Cold War perspective tended to respond to events in highly predictable ways. In Washington and in the American press, for example, Russia's resumption of nuclear testing in the late summer of 1961 frequently was viewed as a vicious attempt to intimidate the West into abandoning its position in Berlin. While this interpretation was plausible, the equally plausible explanation that the Soviets were trying to improve their inferior nuclear technology in the context of the administration's rapid expansion of the American missile force was largely discounted. And yet when the United States resumed testing in the atmosphere the following spring, administration officials and most newspapers considered the move entirely justified. The issue of nuclear fallout, trumpeted during Russia's testing, now was played down or ignored entirely.

The unwillingness or inability to think clearly about how the other side might interpret one's own actions led to the Cuban missile crisis of October 1962, in many ways the climax of the Cold War. American policy toward Cuba between 1960 and 1962 violated every canon of international law and civilized bilateral behavior. The United States sponsored an invasion, including bombing raids, against another sovereign state; it trained and supplied exiles from that nation who, with the knowledge and support of the American government, then conducted repeated raids against Cuba; it engaged in frequent efforts to assassinate Castro; and it canceled all trade with Cuba, and virtually forced some of the countries in Latin America which received American aid to do likewise. Moreover, after the

Bay of Pigs Kennedy made several public statements reaffirming the nation's determination to overthrow the Cuban government. The United States was doing all this and more to oppose a government that did not threaten American security, but which, like the United States, did reserve the right to try to influence developments in other Latin American nations. The Castro government's other major crime was that, partly in response to this unremitting American hostility, it had allied itself ever more closely to the Soviet Union.

Recognizing that Cuba lay within the traditional American sphere of influence, Soviet leaders had accepted an important role there only gradually and, as Herbert S. Dinerstein has noted, with some reluctance. A relatively poor country with no valuable raw materials, Cuba did not offer the prospect of economic gain. Moreover, any Soviet military assistance might well be lost when, as expected, the "imperialists" to the north crushed Castro's revolution the same way the Soviets had eliminated Nagy's in Hungary. And yet Khrushchev, a committed communist, felt some responsibility to assist a nation that was choosing the communist path and thus was furthering the historic transformation of the world from capitalism to communism. And he believed that he had every right under international law to assist another nation in defending itself from attack. If Castro succeeded with Soviet help, the premier could point to Cuba as an example of his effective leadership.

Castro long had taken the American threat to destroy his government very seriously, and after the Bay of Pigs he successfully urged the Soviets to step up the shipments of defensive weapons which could be used to raise the military losses the United States would have to accept if it tried to invade Cuba and overthrow its government. Although Republicans and conservatives complained that Kennedy was "weak" in his dealings with Castro, the administration argued throughout 1961 and 1962 that Cuba had the right to receive "defensive" weapons such as antiaircraft guns and fighter planes—as long as it did not export Soviet weapons to any other nation in the hemisphere. Under strong pressure from Republicans and Cuban exiles, Kennedy in early September 1962 warned that "very grave issues" would arise if the Soviets introduced offensive weapons such as long-range bombers or ground-to-ground missiles. Since such missiles were at that very moment being introduced secretly into Cuba, the stage was set for confrontation as soon as the administration's U-2 flights over the island discovered them on October 14.

After meeting for several days with his advisers and considering options ranging from invading Cuba or bombing the missile sites to proceeding through regular diplomatic channels or even doing nothing, Kennedy dramatically went on national television on Monday, October 22, to reveal the existence of the missiles, to announce the establishment of an American naval "quarantine" (blockade) to prevent the arrival of any additional missiles, and to demand that Khrushchev remove the missiles immediately or face the gravest consequences. During six tense days of military maneuvers, public confrontations, secret diplomacy at the U.N. and in Washington, and statements of support from Allied leaders and of opposition from communist ones, the fate of the world—or at least much of the northern hemisphere—hung in the balance. Soviet leaders naturally wanted to avoid the humiliation of yielding publicly to Kennedy's demands, and proposed that their missiles would be removed from Cuba if American missiles were removed from Turkey.

Kennedy, with his own prestige and his relations with NATO allies on the line, refused to accept such a deal as part of a public agreement. But on Saturday, October 27, his brother Robert assured Soviet ambassador Anatoly Dobrynin that some outmoded U.S. missiles would be removed from Turkey and Italy "within a short time after this crisis was over . . . " With this private assurance and a public agreement that the United States would not invade Cuba, Khrushchev agreed within hours to remove all the missiles. The Cuban missile crisis was over.

Why did the Soviets send the missiles to Cuba? The sinister reason which frequently appeared in the press at the time—that Khrushchev must have been planning a surprise attack against the United States or Latin America—is not convincing, both because he could have attacked from Russia and, more importantly, because he had no desire to subject his country to the devastation of nuclear war. Much more credible is the explanation, corroborated by other Soviet sources, which Khrushchev gave in his memoirs: "The Americans had surrounded our country with military bases and threatened us with nuclear weapons, and now they would learn just what it feels like to have enemy missiles pointed at you."

The need, as Russian leaders saw it in the early 1960s, was to equalize the nuclear arms race, which the United States was winning overwhelmingly, in order to lessen the possibility that America might be tempted to strike first, destroy the Soviet nuclear capability, and suffer relatively little damage in return. And the fastest way to gain greater equality was to introduce medium-range missiles (of which the Soviets had ample supplies) into Cuba, which to the Soviets was the same as Americans having missiles in Western Europe. When Khrushchev persuaded the skeptical Castro in a "very heated" discussion in Moscow in early 1962 that nuclear-tipped missiles should be deployed in Cuba to defend both of their nations, the sequence of events leading to Kennedy's ultimatum was set in motion.

Why did Kennedy pursue the course that he did? After all, in theory he could have accepted the presence of the missiles, which would not have prevented the United States from being able to destroy the Soviet Union in case of nuclear attack. In practice he believed that, given the strong public and congressional sentiment against both Russia and Cuba, he might well have been impeached if he had permitted the missiles to remain. Moreover, operational missiles in Cuba would have undermined the effectiveness of America's early warning systems, and they would have more than doubled the number of missiles the Russians could lay on U.S. targets. Granted that the missiles had to be removed, at least for political reasons and possibly also to maintain respect for American leadership in world affairs, why did Kennedy not tell Soviet leaders privately that removal of the missiles had to begin by a certain date, and that the process had to be completed no later than another date?

This and other options which might have allowed Khrushchev to save face were rejected for a variety of reasons. Especially after the Bay of Pigs, the president harbored an almost obsessive hatred of Castro, and he deeply resented the way Khrushchev had treated him at the Vienna summit. He also was angry that Soviet leaders had assured him repeatedly that no offensive weapons would be introduced into Cuba. Politically, Kennedy was tired of being reminded of his failure at the Bay of Pigs and of being accused during the congressional campaign then in progress of "weakness" in dealing with Castro. As a politician highly sensitive to public opinion, he also was well aware of the strong desire among many Americans in the late 1950s and early 1960s for some kind of clear-cut victory in the Cold War. Finally, as presidential aide Theodore Sorenson noted, Kennedy issued a public ultimatum partly to retain the diplomatic initiative in this delicate situation in which the missiles were rapidly becoming operational and in which the Soviets already had shown considerable duplicity.

In short, by October 1962 Kennedy wanted and believed that he needed a public victory over Khrushchev or Castro, and the circumstances lent considerable justification to a strong stand. Although the way he handled the situation may well have been more dangerous than a private ultimatum would have been, it also afforded the unprecedented opportunity to score a dramatic victory over both of these brash and defiant adversaries at the same time.

Finally, why did Khrushchev back down and agree to remove the missiles? For one thing, Kennedy's approach (unlike the more hawkish bombing proposal) ruled out the killing of Russian soldiers and technicians, at least in the early stages of the crisis, and thus avoided putting Khrushchev in the position of having to avenge the shedding of Russian blood. For another, the apparent proximity of nuclear war affected Khrushchev personally, as when he wrote movingly to Kennedy on October 26 that Russians "are normal people . . . [who] want to live and do not want to destroy your country." Khrushchev also appears to have had genuine respect for Kennedy as an honorable person who wanted peace and one who had the ability to recognize legitimate Soviet interests. "When he gave us public assurances that the U.S. would not organize an invasion of Cuba . . . ," Khrushchev recalled, "we trusted him."

By making the gross miscalculation that the United States would accept the presence of Soviet missiles in Communist Cuba, Khrushchev had flirted with the destruction not only of the missiles and the Russian technicians installing them, but also of Castro's government. And by blockading Cuba and by insisting publicly that Russia remove the missiles under the threat of force, Kennedy was running the risk that the Soviets, for reasons of national pride, would feel compelled to go to war rather than suffer a bitter humiliation. After all, it is an accepted principle in international relations that one nation may assist another in providing for its defense, and indeed the United States had built its anti-communist policy after World War II on just this principle.

In view of the potential for catastrophe inherent in this situation, it is a tribute to both the Soviet and American leaders that they showed sufficient restraint to avoid firing the first shot, to negotiate in good faith in tense circumstances, and finally to pull their nations back from the brink of nuclear war. Without denigrating the diplomacy, one may note that the horror of nuclear war contributed an important element of restraint on both sides. When it became clear within weeks after this sobering experience that both nations were seeking an improved atmosphere, the second dangerous phase of the Cold War was over.

Conclusion

Like the first phase of the Cold War, the second phase from 1953 through 1962 was marked by a huge gap on both sides between the repeatedly expressed desire for world peace and the reality of actions which contributed to East-West tensions. How could the United States, for example, insist on its commitment to world peace and at the same time refuse to let the actual government of the world's most populous nation occupy its country's seat in the United Nations? How could the Soviet Union convince other nations that it respected their independence movements while it was using force to suppress such developments in Eastern Europe? And how could either side, committed to perfecting its nuclear arsenal and (particularly for America) strengthening its military installations and covert operations bases around the globe, convince the other that its intentions were peaceful and defensive?

By the late 1950s and early 1960s, each superpower was running the real danger of becoming overcommitted, of assuming "responsibilities" which it could not fulfill. The Soviet Union was able to limit its involvement in places like Laos and the Congo, but it clearly overreached itself by placing missiles in Cuba. Similarly, the United States might get away with its covert activities in places like British Guiana and Indonesia, but skeptics were asking as early as 1961 and 1962 whether American troops would be any more successful in Vietnam than the French had been a decade earlier. By becoming deeply involved in a nation so close to the United States, Russia was asking for trouble; and by making commitments in an area of the world in which it had no vital interests and acting as if it were Western Europe, America also was courting disaster.

These two key decisions—introducing Soviet missiles into Cuba and U.S. military "advisers" into Vietnam—were made at a time of great tension in East-West relations, and must be viewed in that context. These fateful decisions also were made in the context of heavy domestic pressure on both Khrushchev and Kennedy to achieve some kind of victory in the Cold War. Like other miscalculations in the first dangerous phase, these actions at the height of the second dangerous phase reaffirm the conclusion that leaders of the opposing superpower have been especially prone to serious errors of policy at times in which their bilateral relations already had deteriorated sharply. Whether the leaders were Truman and Stalin or Kennedy and Khrushchev, the combination of hostility abroad and criticism at home could lead to policies in places like Korea, Vietnam, and Cuba which each superpower would come to regret.

But despite the frightening momentum of the Cold War and the double standard for judging international behavior prevalent in both Washington and Moscow, events during the 1950s and early 1960s demonstrated that Soviet-American relations could be conducted at a more civilized level than they had been earlier. The several summit meetings between 1955 and 1961 allowed leaders to get to know each other and to learn which issues each side considered most urgent, and the negotiations on matters ranging from the important issue of arms control to the minor one of airline service between New York and Moscow paved the way for more substantial agreements beginning in 1963. The speed and efficiency with which both formal and informal negotiations were conducted during the week of the Cuban missile crisis suggests the value of the improvement in communications which occurred during the decade after Stalin's death.

In addition to defusing the Cuban crisis, leaders on both sides deserve credit for correctly gauging the other's view of its vital interests and thus avoiding war over such potentially explosive issues as Hungary, Suez, and Berlin. Cold War rhetoric and some actions notwithstanding, after 1953 top leaders in both countries generally were more interested in stabilizing Soviet-American relations than they were in reaching out for clear-cut victories over the other side. This was the reality upon which the two nations would build in the years following the brush with disaster in the fall of 1962.

CHAPTER THREE

The Shift Toward Relative Détente, 1963–1972

In the several decades that have passed since the end of World War II, the years between the resolution of the Cuban missile crisis in late October 1962 and President Nixon's overwhelming reelection in early November 1972 mark the only ten-year period in which Soviet-American relations have shown relatively steady improvement. In addition, Sino-American relations, which during the 1950s and early 1960s had symbolized the gulf separating the "Free World" from the "Communist bloc," improved dramatically after 1969. When Nixon triumphantly visited both Peking and Moscow in the first half of 1972 and pledged the United States to improved relations with both countries, and when Soviet and Chinese officials subsequently visited Washington and toasted détente, the term "cold war" seemed applicable only to an earlier era.

At least as important as particular leaders like Nixon and Russia's Leonid Brezhnev in bringing about the relative détente of these years were international and domestic trends which established conditions conducive to improved East-West relations. There was the bitter Sino-Soviet split, fully public by the end of 1962, which made it in the interest of both countries to seek better relations with the United States in order to lessen the number of either one's enemies. From the American perspective, former CIA official Douglas S. Blaufarb has noted, the open split within the communist movement was the "most momentous" change in the international environment, making it possible for even hard-line U.S. officials to put less emphasis on counterinsurgency by the late 1960s. "Before this development," Blaufarb observed, "the power balance appeared to depend upon containing the threat of monolithic Communism and preventing it from spreading further." There also was an important split within the Western alliance, involving France's veto of Britain's bid to join the Common Market in January 1963, its recognition of mainland China a year later, and its growing independence from NATO in military policy. Other European nations also moved toward expanded political and economic dealings with Russia, China, and East European nations, and the United States faced the choice of getting on the bus or being left behind.

Both the Sino-Soviet and the Franco-American rifts provided clear evidence of the importance of nationalism, of the refusal of nations in either bloc to defer obediently to the wishes of either superpower. And following Khrushchev's removal from power in October 1964, there was an emphasis in the

Kremlin on less "adventurism" in foreign policy and on purchasing Western technology to improve the sluggish Soviet economy, both of which were welcomed by American leaders.

Conditions within the United States also favored East-West détente. By 1963 the American public generally was tired of the bellicose Cold War atmosphere, as both public opinion polls and the response to diplomatic initiatives and conciliatory speeches demonstrated. By the late 1960s a large portion of both the public and the foreign policy establishment was sick of the seemingly endless Vietnam War, and most Americans no longer believed the Cold War clichés that had trumpeted the virtue of ceaseless struggle against communism.

In addition to Vietnam and Johnson's widely criticized intervention in the Dominican Republic in 1965 to prevent "another Cuba," pressing domestic problems such as race relations, inflation, and militant dissent among disaffected young people shifted attention away from superpower relations, and liberals insisted that the nation "reorder its priorities." Moreover, the policy of isolating China was steadily losing ground in both American and international opinion, and many within the business community believed that restrictions on trade with Russia and Eastern Europe were untenable at a time when the United States was no longer as dominant in the international economy as it had been in the 1940s and 1950s. Despite continuing suspicion of Russia and China, therefore, most Americans supported concrete steps toward improving East-West relations. The stage was set for the most constructive period in great power diplomacy in recent memory.

An Improved Atmosphere in 1963

The last year of Kennedy's presidency was a watershed in Soviet-American relations. In addition to the "Treaty Banning Nuclear Weapons Tests in the Atmosphere, in Outer Space and Under Water" signed in Moscow in August 1963, the two nations made a number of lesser agreements, including the installation of a "hot line" between the White House and the Kremlin to facilitate communications in times of crisis. In a move which served as a precedent for subsequent large-scale business deals, Kennedy in October 1963 approved the sale, through private channels, of $250 million worth of surplus American wheat to Russia. In a letter to Congress justifying his action, the president emphasized the practical point that "such sales will strengthen farm prices in the United States and bring added income and employment to American shipping, longshoremen and railroad workers as well as grain traders and farmers." Noting the improved atmosphere, a reporter covering Soviet-American relations observed on October 3 that "the discussion has now been brought down from the realm of ideology to the familiar precincts of traditional diplomacy."

Although advocates of nuclear disarmament would have preferred an agreement banning underground testing as well, the test ban treaty still was a significant first step toward bringing the nuclear arms race under at least modest control. The signers eventually included more than one hundred nations, including the three major nuclear powers at the time—the United States, Britain, and Russia—but not France and China, both in the early stages of developing their nuclear capabilities. Atmospheric testing by the two superpowers had increased Cold War tensions and caused environmental damage from the mid-1940s through the early 1960s, and these in themselves were sufficient reasons to applaud the treaty. But its larger significance was that it demonstrated, after years of failure and disappointment, that the two sides were capable of achieving specific agreements in the emotion-charged area of defense policy. By undercutting the argument of hard liners on both sides that the only choice was to arm to the teeth and prepare for Armageddon, the successful negotiations made it possible to think in terms of additional agreements to bring some predictability to the arms race.

A key development along the road to signing the treaty was a speech Kennedy gave at American University on June 10, 1963. In a tone far more conciliatory than is found in his major addresses of 1961 and 1962, the president told the graduating seniors that "both the United States and its allies, and the Soviet Union and its allies, have a mutually deep interest in a just and genuine peace and in halting the arms race." He urged Americans to "reexamine our attitude toward the cold war"; the time had come "not to see only a distorted and desperate view of the other side, not to see conflict as inevitable, accommodation as impossible, and communication as nothing more than an exchange of threats."

Kennedy reminded his listeners of Soviet sacrifices in World War II, of Russia's numerous achievements, and of the fact that the two nations had never been at war; yet "we are both caught up in a vicious and dangerous cycle in which suspicion on one side breeds suspicion on the other, and new weapons breed counterweapons." Promising that the United States "will never start a war," the president urged Soviet leaders to work with him to break this cycle, and he outlined specific steps the United States was taking to facilitate the completion of a test ban treaty.

Kennedy's speech and his appointment of the respected Averell Harriman to head the nation's negotiating team were taken in Moscow as signs of American seriousness in seeking a test ban treaty. The speech was reprinted in full in Soviet newspapers; some Russians, as tired of the Cold War as were many Americans, carried clippings of the speech in their wallets for months as a symbol of the improved East-West atmosphere. The president continued his largely conciliatory approach to the Soviets until his assassination that November. At the United Nations on September 29, for example, he applauded the "pause in the Cold War," urged "further agreements" to slow the arms race, and insisted that "the badge of responsibility in the modern world is a willingness to seek peaceful solutions." Although Kennedy balanced his speeches with reminders that "basic differences" in outlook still remained, his approach was far more conducive to improved relations than it had been in previous years.

Khrushchev, for his part, was anxious to improve relations with the West at a time of intense Sino-Soviet hostility. The Russians needed a positive achievement to balance the humiliation in Cuba the previous fall, and they also needed concrete agreements with the West to demonstrate to other communist parties that their policy of peaceful coexistence was more beneficial than Peking's outspoken insistence on hostility toward the capitalist nations. Far behind the West in nuclear missiles and bombers, the Russians needed time to move toward equality in strategic weapons before risking another confrontation with the United States. As Soviet Deputy Foreign Minister Vassily Kuznetsov bitterly warned U.S. diplomat John McCloy shortly after the missile crisis, "You Americans will never be able to do this to us again." Most important, the Russians needed agreements with the West in order to ensure that they would be able to meet the challenge from their populous enemy in the East. Indeed, negotiations in Moscow between Russia and China broke off— without any progress toward resolving outstanding issues—on July 21, just four days before Soviet, British, and American negotiators completed the test ban treaty.

The abrupt shift in the international atmosphere contributed to a debate within the United States about what its implications were, and about what additional steps, if any, should be taken. Young liberals seemed most willing to plunge ahead to try to end the Cold War: a group of students defied the official ban on travel to Cuba in the summer of 1963, and the Young Democrats of California resolved in September that the United States should recognize mainland China, improve relations with Cuba and East Germany, and withdraw its forces from Vietnam. At the other end of the political spectrum, conservatives tried to prevent Senate ratification of the Test Ban Treaty (it passed, 80 to 19, on September 24), criticized the grain deal with Russia, and denounced Kennedy in October for holding talks in the White House with a communist leader, Tito, while refusing to meet with a member of South Vietnam's ruling family. Once started, where would the relaxation of tensions end, conservative journalists asked nervously. Would Kennedy next follow the Canadian example and sell grain to China? Would he seek to establish relations with Cuba?

When asked such questions at press conferences, Kennedy generally denied any change in policy toward other communist nations, and he explicitly disassociated himself from the Young Democrats' resolutions. Kennedy already viewed Goldwater as his likely opponent in the 1964 election, and he did not want to risk losing the middle ground in foreign policy to him. But there is considerable evidence that the president was thinking seriously about shifting U.S. policy on China and Vietnam—if not on Cuba—after his probable reelection. Roger Hilsman and some others at the State Department worked on developing a policy of greater flexibility toward China during 1962 and 1963, and Kennedy said at his last press conference on November 14, 1963, that the administration was "not wedded to a policy of hostility to Red China." When Quaker leaders visiting with Kennedy in the White House that summer urged him to improve relations with China, Kennedy listened sympathetically and responded, "You light a fire under me, and I'll move on it."

Similarly, Kennedy told Senator Mike Mansfield in early 1963 that he planned a complete military withdrawal from Vietnam after the election. "If I tried to pull out completely now, we would have another Joe McCarthy red scare on our hands, but I can do it after I'm reelected," he explained to presidential aide Kenneth O'Donnell after Mansfield departed. "So we had better make damned sure that I am reelected." Although he insisted publicly throughout 1963 that the United States should not abandon its commitment in Vietnam, Kennedy apparently made comments similar to those he made to Mansfield and O'Donnell to presidential aide Michael Forrestal and to dovish Senator Wayne Morse in the fall of 1963.

To note that Kennedy was thinking about changing America's Cold War policies in Asia does not prove that he would have done so if he had lived and been reelected. What he might have done is a moot point. But it does suggest that, in the context of the administration's new self-confidence after the Cuban missile crisis, Kennedy was considering a shift away from some policies which had seemed appropriate in the frigid atmosphere of 1961. If so, his cautious, private shift on Asian policy may be seen as paralleling his emphatic, public shift on policy toward Russia.

Unfortunately, Kennedy did not share his private thoughts on Asia with his vice-president, Lyndon Johnson, who was considered a "cold warrior" and with whom, in any case, the president did not have a close personal relationship. As with Truman in April 1945, the new president who took power in November 1963 was relatively inexperienced in foreign affairs and ill-informed about the intricacies of his predecessor's policies.

Vietnam at Center Stage, 1964–1968

Although other issues existed, the five-year Johnson presidency was dominated by race relations at home and Vietnam abroad. On the one, Johnson reacted with both compassion and substantial effectiveness; on the other, he responded with neither imagination nor common sense. His policy of sharply escalating the American military involvement in Indochina, after running as a man of peace in the 1964 election, alienated many liberals, and his apparent determination to pursue victory in Vietnam regardless of the consequences alienated allies in Western Europe and strained relations with Russia and China. But this was by no means a totally negative period in East-West relations, for both America and Russia were interested in maintaining at least some of the momentum for improved relations begun in 1963, and pressures built within the United States to try to develop a more constructive policy toward Peking.

Why did Johnson and his chief foreign policy advisers— Secretary of State Dean Rusk, Secretary of Defense Robert McNamara, and national security adviser McGeorge Bundy— decide in early 1965 to begin bombing North Vietnam and to send substantial numbers of American combat troops to fight in South Vietnam? Although the administration frequently deceived the public and withheld information about specific military operations (e.g., the Gulf of Tonkin incident off North Vietnam in August 1964 and the secret bombing of Laos from the mid-1960s through the early 1970s), it was quite open about the basic reasons for its large-scale intervention in Indochina. In its view, it was doing precisely what Eisenhower and Kennedy had done in the late 1950s and early 1960s: helping the South Vietnamese government defeat the Communist insurgents, thereby demonstrating that America "keeps its commitments" and that "aggression doesn't pay." More broadly, it was following the Cold War policy of containing communism and upholding what it considered to be the proper balance of power in Southeast Asia.

Perhaps the clearest statements of the administration's position were contained in a speech Johnson gave at Johns Hopkins University on April 17, 1965, and in a special message to Congress four weeks later. "Our objective is the independence of South Viet-Nam, and its freedom from attack," Johnson said in his speech. "We want nothing for ourselves—only that the people of South Viet-Nam be allowed to guide their own country in their own way." American intervention was justified because "North Viet-Nam has attacked the independent nation of South Viet-Nam" and because North Vietnam's leaders "are urged on by Peking." In the president's view, the stakes were much larger than simply the fate of South Vietnam: people from West Berlin to Thailand counted on America's keeping its commitments. "The aim [of the communists] in Viet-Nam is not simply the conquest of the South, tragic as that would be," Johnson asserted in his message to Congress asking for $700 million in additional appropriations for the war. "It is to show that the American commitment is worthless. Once that is done, the gates are down and the road is open to expansion and endless conquest." Citing the Cold War experience in places like Iran, Greece, and Korea, the president insisted that "the American people . . . have learned the great lesson of this generation: wherever we have stood firm aggression has been halted, peace restored and liberty maintained."

The largest error Johnson and his advisers made in the spring of 1965 was to base their policy less on the concrete realities of the situation in Vietnam and the marginal American interests there than on the alleged aims of international communism and on painful memories of past experiences at home and abroad. Given the Sino-Soviet split and Ho Chi Minh's nationalist brand of communism, to speak of an international communist movement bent on "endless conquest" showed very limited insight into the situation in Vietnam. The communist leadership in Hanoi capitalized on the long-standing determination of Vietnamese nationalists to end foreign domination, and on the general perception of the Americans as colonial successors to the French. The U.S.-backed government in Saigon suffered from the overwhelming American presence, and tried vainly to compensate by sheer military force for what it lacked in political appeal. In this situation Ho Chi Minh and his colleagues, although quite dependent on aid from both Russia and China, were nevertheless the only credible liberators of Vietnam in the eyes of increasing numbers of their compatriots. Their objective, widely shared, was to remove American power from South Vietnam and, presumably, to unite the country.

Johnson's Cold War mentality and fear of renewed McCarthyism as influences on his policy in 1965 emerged graphically in a subsequent interview with political scientist Doris Kearns:

. . . everything I knew about history told me that if I got out of Vietnam and let Ho Chi Minh run through the streets of Saigon, then I'd be doing exactly what Chamberlain [British prime minister in the late 1930s, who became the symbol of appeasement] did in World War II. I'd be giving a big fat reward to aggression. And I knew that if we let Communist aggression succeed in taking over South Vietnam, there would follow in this country an endless national debate . . . that would shatter my Presidency, kill my administration, and damage our democracy. I knew that Harry Truman and Dean Acheson had lost their effectiveness from the day that the Communists took over China. I believed that the loss of China had played a large role in the rise of Joe McCarthy. And I knew that all these problems, taken together, were chickenshit compared with what might happen if we lost Vietnam.

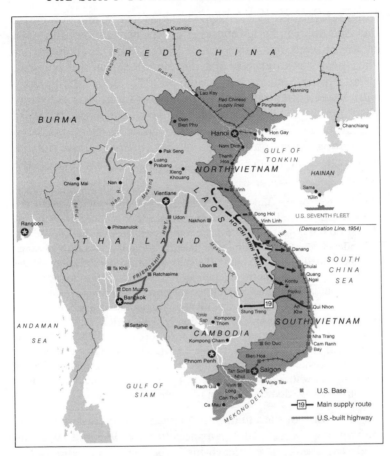

Most critics of the American intervention did not question Johnson's sincerity, and they also acknowledged that there had been times and places in which American firmness in defense of Western interests had been justified. Many even supported the sending of American weapons and economic aid to the South Vietnamese government in the hope that this assistance would foster reforms, promote village-level democracy, and thus create the solid political base which that government lacked. But most critics believed that large-scale, direct American military involvement was a mistake, that the administration was plunging ahead on the basis of faulty premises. To many, the analogy with Korea, often cited by the administration, was especially misleading. The *New Republic,* for example, viewed the intervention in Korea as justified to check Soviet aggression "operating through a puppet" North Korean regime. But the historical circumstances in Vietnam were "very nearly the reverse":

On the heels of the Japanese surrender, the Vietnamese assumed the right of self-determination and declared the independence of Vietnam. If they do not now fully possess the right of self-determination and enjoy independence as a nation it is because of actions taken by France and the United States. Pleading the cause of self-determination for the Vietnamese in the South (excluding those who refuse to accept a government installed and maintained under a foreign shield—they have no rights) we have deprived the Vietnamese people as a whole of that right and preserved an artificial division of their nation. . . .

We have sent an army to Vietnam to force a settlement of a civil war on our terms, and we have done so without any mandate from any government that could conceivably be regarded as representative of Vietnam and without any mandate from the international community. . . . what we have done in Vietnam is to commit aggression.

This view of the situation in Vietnam was increasingly common among liberals and Asian specialists by 1965 and 1966. Indeed, the speakers at "teach-ins" about the war and rallies against the war often made precisely these points. In their view, the tragedy was not simply that the Johnson administration was misguided in its heavy-handed policies, but rather that the entire thrust of American policy toward Vietnam since World War II had been wrongheaded and perhaps evil. It had been wrong to aid the French in trying to maintain their Indochina colonies, to assist in setting up a separate government in Saigon, to send the CIA and American military "advisers" to shore up this corrupt and dictatorial regime, and now to dispatch the latest in American military technology (except for nuclear weapons) to blow up and burn helpless civilians as well as those who understandably opposed U.S. policies. And if the United States had been so consistently opposed to allowing the Vietnamese to establish their independence and work out their own internal affairs, then perhaps the entire American policy toward developing nations since the beginning of the Cold War required a searching reexamination.

The collapse of the Cold War consensus, to which Johnson and Rusk still appealed, occurred on several levels. There was what might be called polite dissent, which involved raising questions and expressing concerns about American policy in Asia without challenging most earlier Cold War policies. Many of the academics and former officials who testified at the Senate hearings on Vietnam and on China in 1966 would fit roughly in this category, as would respected senators like J. William Fulbright (Dem., Arkansas) and newspapers like the *New York Times*. Then there was insistent dissent, like that found in the pages of the liberal magazines or in meetings of liberal organizations like Americans for Democratic Action, which strongly opposed the war and supported American recognition of mainland China. And finally there was uncompromising dissent, to be heard at antiwar rallies and to be read in publications of Students for a Democratic Society and other left-wing organizations. To these critics on the socialist left, the fundamental problem was capitalism, and Vietnam was only one example of what capitalist nations would do to destroy socialist movements and protect potential markets and sources of raw materials.

Ignoring its strident opponents, the Johnson administration responded to its moderate critics in Congress and in the press by insisting that they were entirely wrong about Vietnam, that it was necessary to stand firm there to demonstrate America's resolve to defend freedom wherever it was threatened. The administration was not clear about precisely who the enemy was—North Vietnam, China, or simply communism—but it was determined to defeat it. And regarding the calls for better relations with China, the administration insisted by 1966 that it was initiating modest first steps to improve relations, but that the Chinese were responding with unrelenting hostility. In taking these Cold War stands, the Democratic administration could count on strong but increasingly silent support from Republicans and conservative Democrats in Congress, who together assured passage of all appropriations bills to cover the burgeoning costs of the war.

While consistently escalating the war in Vietnam until March 1968, the administration pursued a contradictory policy toward China. On the one hand, it made conciliatory overtures, as in Hilsman's speech in San Francisco in December 1963 and Johnson's call in April 1965 for a "freer flow of ideas and people between mainland China and the United States." Both publicly and in meetings with Chinese representatives in Warsaw, the administration assured Peking that its objectives in Asia were limited and that it favored increased contacts between the two countries.

On the other hand, the administration warned the public that a China armed with even primitive nuclear weapons —it conducted its first nuclear test in August 1964—was a greater threat than Russia; it insisted on keeping Taiwan in the United Nations and maintaining its defense arrangements with Chiang Kai-shek's government; and it repeatedly implied that China was the prime culprit in Vietnam. High officials like Rusk and national security adviser Walt Rostow harbored a long-standing hatred of China, and Rusk in particular went out of his way to insult the proud Chinese by repeatedly referring to their capital by its former name, "Peiping." In his memoirs, Johnson referred to China only in negative terms, failed to mention any American initiatives for better relations, and advanced the fanciful notion that China in 1965 was on the verge of dominating the entire region by means of a "Djakarta-Hanoi-Peking-Pyongyang axis."

Even if the administration had sent more consistently conciliatory signals to Peking, it is not clear that relations could have been improved as long as the United States was expanding its military involvement along China's southern border. In their public statements Chinese leaders expressed the fear that America might widen the war to include their country, and they warned the United States that an invasion of North Vietnam would lead to Chinese intervention. In the mid-1960s China sent modest amounts of military and economic aid to North Vietnam, and Chinese and American warplanes occasionally exchanged fire and inflicted casualties in or near Chinese air space. Despite such incidents, the Johnson administration avoided the kinds of provocations which had led to the large-scale Chinese intervention in Korea fifteen years before.

China's militant verbal support for world revolution, the principal ideological underpinning for its feud with Russia, also hindered Sino-American rapprochement. The same American officials who had been worried in 1961 about Khrushchev's support for "wars of national liberation" found confirmation for America's hard-line stance in Vietnam in Lin Piao's statement in 1965 advocating "people's war" in developing nations in order to defeat "U.S. imperialism and its lackeys." As this statement suggests, the rhetoric pouring forth from Peking between 1963 and 1968 was as bitterly anti-American as ever, and the Cultural Revolution, beginning in 1966, caused so much turmoil within China that serious Sino-American negotiations probably could not have occurred even under more favorable international circumstances at least until 1968. From the administration's viewpoint, the Chinese seemed as determined to remain isolated from the United States as they were to perpetuate their bitter feud with Russia.

Although the Soviet Union sent military aid to North Vietnam, especially after the bombing of the north began in 1965, neither side allowed Soviet-American relations to deteriorate to anything approaching the continuing hostility in Sino-American relations. Johnson and Rusk wanted to maintain the process of patient negotiations with Russia which had borne fruit in the summer of 1963, and Khrushchev's successors in late 1964— party leader Leonid Brezhnev and Premier Alexei Kosygin—also were interested in improved relations with the West. While

American leaders were anxious to demonstrate that the Vietnam War was not blocking progress toward détente with Russia, Soviet leaders had to be careful not to give the appearance that they were selling out the interests of a beleaguered communist nation, North Vietnam, in order to further their relationship with Washington. The result was a more subdued and cautious process of accommodation than might have occurred without the American escalation in Vietnam, but one which still yielded fairly significant results.

When Soviet-American relations have been acrimonious, as they were in 1950 and 1961, American leaders have tended to use their nation's superior wealth and technology to improve their position in the strategic arms race. When these relations have been fairly conciliatory, as they were between 1963 and the early 1970s, the emphasis has been less on winning the race than on setting limits to it. This period saw two important U.S. initiatives in the latter direction: a treaty, initiated in 1964 and signed in 1968 by many nations, including Russia and America, to prevent the spread of nuclear weapons to nations other than the five that already had them; and an effort, started in 1967, to limit the number of offensive intercontinental ballistic missiles (ICBMs) and defensive antiballistic missiles (ABMs) which each side could deploy. Although the strategic-missile and ABM agreements (known together as SALT I) were not signed until 1972, the Johnson administration began the negotiating process which led to them.

One reason Soviet leaders were cautious in responding to American initiatives on arms control was that, until the late 1960s, Russia was well behind the United States in offensive strategic weapons. Although Brezhnev and Kosygin wanted improved Soviet-American relations, they also were determined to end the gross disparity between the two sides' nuclear capabilities, thus lessening the likelihood of another humiliation such as occurred during the Cuban missile crisis and achieving international acceptance of Russia as the full strategic equal of America. As late as 1965, Russia had an estimated 262 ICBMs to America's 854, 155 strategic bombers to America's 738, and zero submarine-based missiles to America's 464. As a result of American restraint after 1967 and its own efforts to achieve parity, by 1969 Russia actually led in ICBMs, 1,198 to 1,054, though it trailed in the number of warheads these missiles could carry, 1,326 to 1,710. While the West maintained a comfortable lead in deliverable warheads during the 1970s, the Soviets were close enough to equality to enter into arms control negotiations with reasonable confidence.

Johnson boasted in his memoirs that America and Russia signed a larger number of "significant agreements" during his presidency than they had in the previous thirty years. The proud Texan habitually exaggerated, but it is true that the two nations concluded a steady stream of modest agreements which helped to maintain the constructive atmosphere in Soviet-American relations. There was a treaty formalizing the pledges of the two nations not to station nuclear weapons in space; there was the U.S.-Soviet Consular Convention, which facilitated travel and other activities in each country; and there were agreements on such diverse subjects as returning astronauts who might accidentally land on foreign soil and prescribing what Soviet and American fishing fleets had a right to catch in each other's territorial waters. The cultural exchange agreement was renewed in 1964 despite some pressure in both countries to cancel it, and roughly 16,000 American tourists visited Russia in 1966. None of these things by itself was especially earthshaking, but all of them together, combined with progress on arms control and relative Soviet restraint on Vietnam, suggested a more constructive and stable relationship than the two superpowers had experienced since World War II.

The fact that crises in the Middle East in 1967 and in Czechoslovakia the next year did not lead to wider conflict underscored the value of the generally positive atmosphere in Soviet-American relations. Tensions had been rising in the Middle East between Israel, heavily backed by the U.S. government and most American Jewish organizations, and Egypt and Syria, armed by Russia. In May 1967 President Nasser of Egypt, amid signs of impending hostilities between Israel and his ally Syria, closed the Gulf of Aqaba to Israeli shipping and obtained the removal of the U.N. peace-keeping force which ever since the 1956 invasion had patrolled Egyptian territory in the Sinai along the Israeli border. Both Russia and America feared the outbreak of a war which they could not control and which might lead to superpower confrontation; and, while the Russians were urging caution on Nasser, both Johnson and French President Charles de Gaulle (a supplier of aircraft to Israel) were admonishing Israel to show restraint. De Gaulle, who earlier had urged Kennedy not to make the same mistake France had made in becoming involved militarily in Indochina, told Israeli Foreign Minister Abba Eban that his nation should not start a war. "You will be considered the aggressor by the world and by me," the French leader warned. "You will cause the Soviet Union to penetrate more deeply into the Middle East, and Israel will suffer the consequences. You will create a Palestinian nationalism, and you will never be able to get rid of it."

Spurning all this advice and not informing Washington of its plans, Israel made an effective surprise attack on Egypt and Syria on June 5, 1967. Within six days it had won a smashing victory over those two nations and Jordan, and seized large chunks of their territory. During the fighting Johnson and Kosygin used the "hot line" to exchange assurances of nonbelligerency, and Johnson carefully informed the Russians in advance about American troop movements in the area, as in the aftermath of Israel's accidental sinking of an American warship. After the end of the Six Day War Russian leaders backed the Arabs in angrily denouncing Israel's refusal to withdraw from the lands conquered during the fighting, and they also found themselves having to replace much of the military equipment lost by Egypt and Syria in the war. But, as de Gaulle had warned, Russian influence in the region increased, for the United States appeared to many Arabs as an accomplice in Israel's conquests.

Despite the situation in the Middle East and the continued heavy American involvement in Vietnam, Kosygin accepted an invitation to meet with Johnson in late June 1967 at a college in

Glassboro, New Jersey, to discuss current world problems. Although the meetings between the two leaders were cordial, it was a measure of the element of strain in Soviet-Amerîcan relations during the Vietnam War that Kosygin had refused to hold the meetings with Johnson either in Washington or at Camp David.

This Soviet reticence diminished after the signing of the nonproliferation treaty on July 1, 1968. Within weeks of that event, Soviet leaders invited Johnson to come to Russia in early October to inaugurate formal talks on strategic arms limitation. After discussing the invitation with Rusk and Rostow on August 19, the president decided to accept, and to issue a news release on the subject two days later. On August 20, however, on learning that Soviet troops had invaded Czechoslovakia Johnson felt compelled to postpone planning for the visit to Russia and to go on national television to denounce the Soviet move and to demand the withdrawal of all Warsaw Pact forces.

The Soviets invaded Czechoslovakia for many of the same reasons that had led them to crush the rebellion in Hungary twelve years before. During the spring and summer of 1968 a new Czech government under Alexander Dubcek had been acceding to popular demands for broadening civil liberties, allowing greater freedom of the press, and permitting non-communists to participate more actively in politics. From the Russian viewpoint, the events in Czechoslovakia threatened the continuation of the communist system not only there, but also in other East European countries and in Russia itself. Regrettably, as John Lewis Gaddis has observed, "the Warsaw pact simply could not accommodate the diversities of viewpoint, and hence of political systems, that characterized its Western counterpart."

Although Soviet purposes in 1956 and 1968 were quite similar, both their approach and the U.S. response were more restrained than in the Cold War atmosphere of 1956. They took the trouble this time to bring units from East Germany, Poland, and Hungary with them—a demonstration of Warsaw Pact solidarity. Also in contrast to Hungary, the Soviets knew in advance that the Czechs would not offer significant armed resistance to a military intervention. Finally, through a special meeting between Ambassador Dobrynin and President Johnson, Russian leaders made a point of assuring the president of the importance they attached to constructive relations with the United States.

By the mid-1960s the American government had shifted its basic policy toward Eastern Europe from urging "liberation" by dissidents in each country—a policy whose unreality had been fully revealed in 1956—to "building bridges" of trade and cooperation with the increasingly independent communist governments there. This fundamental departure affected America's response in 1968. Although the administration welcomed the liberalization in Czechoslovakia, it carefully avoided depicting the situation in Cold War terminology until after the actual invasion. Even then, its reaction, though sharp, was brief—unlike the years of diplomatic ostracism of Hungary after 1956. Within a few months after the invasion the administration was anxious to get on with the SALT negotiations. Johnson, who had invested considerable effort and political capital in improving Soviet-American relations, felt rebuffed when the Kremlin turned down his offer in late November to meet with Soviet leaders in Geneva before Christmas. The Russians apparently had decided that it would be prudent to wait until after the new Republican administration assumed power in January 1969.

Toward a New Balance of Power, 1969–1972

American foreign policy from 1969 until the mid-1970s was directed by two bold, controversial leaders, President Richard Nixon and his chief national security adviser, Henry Kissinger. A native Californian and opportunistic politician, Nixon rose to national prominence as an opponent of domestic communists and liberals during the late 1940s, and he was known during his eight years as Eisenhower's vice-president as a staunch "cold warrior." Although he was defeated for the presidency in 1960 and for governor of California in 1962, Nixon returned to prominence in the Republican party after Barry Goldwater's defeat in 1964 by campaigning tirelessly in behalf of GOP candidates and by emphasizing his middle-of-the-road position within the party. When the Democratic party splintered in 1968 under the strains of Vietnam and domestic polarization, Nixon was able to mount a successful campaign for the White House. His remark in 1969 that "flexibility is the first principle of politics" was clearly exemplified in his foreign policy—especially by the startling shift in his approach to Russia and China during his presidency.

If Nixon is best viewed as an ambitious, amoral politician, Kissinger may be considered an ambitious political scientist more interested in influencing decision-making in Washington than in teaching students or writing scholarly books. A Jew born in Germany and educated at Harvard, Kissinger could hardly have been more different from Nixon in background. Indeed, until the 1968 election Kissinger was best known in Republican circles as a protégé of and adviser to Nixon's arch rival, Governor Nelson Rockefeller of New York. But Nixon and Kissinger shared an interest in broad conceptual approaches to foreign policy, and both spent considerable time during the Kennedy-Johnson years reflecting upon the limits of the Cold War approach in dealing with the major communist powers. In an article in *Foreign Affairs* in October 1967, for example, Nixon noted that "the role of the United States as a policeman is likely to be limited in the future," and argued that "we simply cannot afford to leave China forever outside the family of nations . . ." Such public comments from the leader of the Republican party would have been unthinkable a decade before.

As John G. Stoessinger has pointed out, Kissinger's conception of great power politics was based on three main assumptions: first, to quote Stoessinger, "to be secure, a peace must be based on a negotiated settlement, with all sides in equilibrium, rather than on a victor's peace"; second, the leading power (in this case, the United States) must give the chief rival power (in this case, Russia) a tangible stake in improved relations; and third, to maitain equilibrium or balance in the system, a bal-

ancer is required to "throw his weight on the weaker side whenever an imbalance occurs and by so doing restore the equilibrium
and maintain the peace." In Kissinger's view, America should
play the key role of balancer, working to increase Russia's stake
in the international system while simultaneously increasing
China's ability to serve as a counterweight to Russian influence
in Asia. In addition to America, Russia, and China, a resurgent
Europe and Japan completed the pentagonal structure of power.
Reflecting this viewpoint, Nixon remarked in late 1971 that
"it will be a safer world if we have a strong, healthy United
States, Europe, Soviet Union, China, Japan, each balancing the
other . . ."

Recognizing that America's power was more limited than it
had been in the late 1940s, Nixon and Kissinger sought to establish a "structure of peace" in which common interests and
incentives for conciliatory behavior would be emphasized, and
ideology and instinctive hostility—so important in the thinking
of John Foster Dulles and Mao Tse-tung in the 1950s—would be
played down. Convinced that both Russia and China would
have to play a constructive role if this new balance of power was
to succeed, the Nixon administration moved toward better relations with both countries, thus transforming the Cold War. But
while they achieved many of their goals in foreign policy, the
new leaders' decision to continue the Vietnam War, combined
with the unlawful means they often used against their domestic
opponents, ironically contributed to a result these proponents of
presidential power abhorred: an increase in the ability and determination of Congress and other institutions in American society
to influence the nation's foreign policies.

Before elaborating on the Nixon administration's success in
easing tensions with Russia and China, some discussion of its
less successful policy in Indochina seems appropriate. While
domestic issues were important, Nixon also was elected in 1968
because of the public's disillusionment with the war. In September 1964, shortly before Johnson's landslide victory over Goldwater, Gallup's respondents had viewed the Democrats as the

party best able to maintain peace by the margin of 43 to 20 percent. Due to the escalation in Vietnam, the Republicans had taken an eight-point lead by June 1966, and the month before the 1968 election they led by 37 to 24 percent. During the campaign Nixon naturally encouraged the view that the Republicans could end the war, and he claimed that he had a plan for doing so, which he would implement if elected. Neither supporters nor opponents of the war knew what Nixon's plan was, however, because he refused to discuss details on the grounds that he did not want to jeopardize the negotiations which recently had begun in Paris.

Upon his inauguration Nixon had a golden opportunity to end the direct American military involvement in Vietnam, either immediately or in a phased withdrawal to be completed within a few months. The president could have announced that America had done all that anyone reasonably could expect it to do, and he could have quoted Kennedy's remark in September 1963 that success in the war ultimately depended upon South Vietnam's performance and not America's military assistance. Instead, Nixon tragically became the fifth consecutive American president determined to prevent a communist victory in Vietnam's civil war.

Like his four predecessors, Nixon was more concerned about the possible impact of failure to "help" Vietnam on conditions in America and elsewhere than he was about the situation in Vietnam itself. As he told a journalist in May 1969, "We would destroy ourselves if we pulled out in a way that wasn't really honorable." Kissinger agreed, noting in an article that same year that "what is involved now is confidence in American promises." In an article in the *New Republic* in August 1980, Kissinger acknowledged that he had been wrong in 1966 to advocate a continuation of the war, that the United States probably should have cut its losses and gotten out. But when they took office, Nixon and Kissinger reiterated the stale Cold War view that America had to remain in Vietnam until "peace with honor" was achieved.

What the new leaders in Washington seemed unable to understand was that, by the late 1960s, the Viet Cong and the North Vietnamese had made too many sacrifices—and had too good a prospect of winning—to be willing to end the war by accepting the legitimacy of the American-backed South Vietnamese government. In their view, America could have peace by withdrawing its forces, or it could seek to defend its honor by remaining in Vietnam. But no matter how much it bombed and threatened, it could not achieve peace with honor, as Nixon defined the phrase. In a letter to the president in August 1969, shortly before his death, Ho Chi Minh said that he was "deeply touched at the rising toll of death of young Americans who have fallen in Vietnam by reason of the policy of American governing circles." But he insisted that if the United States wanted to "act for a just peace," it would have to "cease the war of aggression and withdraw their troops from South Vietnam, and respect the right of the population of the South and of the Vietnamese nation to dispose of themselves, without foreign influence." As former U.S. official Townsend Hoopes observed in 1970, "The one thing we can negotiate at this stage of the war is the manner of our going."

After four years of intense fighting and domestic controversy under Johnson, numerous public opinion polls showed that most Americans by 1969–1970 were anxious to have the war ended, even if the United States lost. But Nixon gave them exactly four more years of war: direct American military involvement ended when the so-called peace agreements were signed in January 1973. Although he was under substantial domestic pressure to end the war quickly, Nixon tried bolder and riskier tactics than Johnson had used to try to force the Viet Cong and the North Vietnamese to give up the fight. Nixon tried to threaten Hanoi into suing for peace in 1969, and he also told Russian leaders that progress toward détente depended upon their success in getting the North Vietnamese to accede to American demands. When these and other gambits failed, the president asserted that his policy of "Vietnamization"—turning over more of the ground fighting to the South Vietnamese while gradually withdrawing U.S. troops—was succeeding.

Apparently unconcerned about civilian casualties, Nixon repeatedly ordered intense bombing raids in South Vietnam, North Vietnam, Laos, and, for the first time, Cambodia. While claiming that he was winding down the war, he infuriated his critics by dropping more tons of bombs throughout Indochina in four years than Johnson had done, by sending American troops into Cambodia in 1970, and by mining the harbor at Haiphong and carpet-bombing suburbs of Hanoi two years later. While Nixon and Kissinger were protecting America's "honor," an additional 20,553 American soldiers were killed, an estimated one million Indochinese soldiers and civilians were killed, and millions more were wounded or turned into refugees. In Western Europe and elsewhere, the United States under Johnson and Nixon was gaining a reputation for ruthlessness and disregard for international opinion totally inconsistent with its earlier image as protector of the free world.

While Nixon's hard-nosed policies in Indochina may have won him some support among the so-called "silent majority," who were tired of the radicalism and turmoil in America in the mid to late 1960s, his administration clearly had a domestic price to pay for continuing the war long after it had lost the degree of support required in a democracy to sustain a viable military involvement abroad. The administration was confronted with widespread draft resistance and repeated peaceful demonstrations involving hundreds of thousands of Americans at a time, and it also faced a small minority determined to "bring the war home." Groups like the radical "Weathermen" faction of Students for a Democratic Society were responsible for bombings, broken windows, and other efforts to "trash" the establishment and hence to show solidarity with the Viet Cong and other Third World liberation movements. More significantly, Congress was increasingly assertive, especially after the unexpected "incursion" into Cambodia led to nationwide protests and the killing of student demonstrators at Kent State University in Ohio and Jackson State University in Mississippi. In the wake of the invasion of Cambodia, the Senate repealed the Gulf of Tonkin Resolution of 1964, which had given the president the authority to wage war in Southeast Asia; and it also passed a watered-down version of a proposal to prohibit spending on military operations in Cambodia. Johnson's and Nixon's high-handed policies in Indochina led in 1973 to passage of the War Powers Act, which limited to sixty days the president's right to commit troops abroad without congressional approval.

Finally, the Nixon-Kissinger policies in Indochina contributed, at least indirectly, to the series of illegal activities which became known simply as "Watergate." Irritated by leaks to the press in the spring of 1969 about the secret bombing of Cambodia, the administration began wiretapping the home phone of Morton Halperin, an official on Kissinger's National Security Council staff. Subsequently, the wiretapping included respected journalists, including columnists Joseph Kraft and Jack Anderson, who were publishing information on foreign affairs that was embarrassing to the administration. In the summer of 1971, after former official Daniel Ellsberg released the government's secret history of the Vietnam war to the press, the White House took the step which led directly to the incident at Watergate a year later: it established a secret dirty-tricks group called the "plumbers," composed largely of former CIA operatives. On September 4, 1971, members of this group conducted an illegal break-in at the office of Ellsberg's psychiatrist, Dr. Lewis Fielding, in order to try to locate material to discredit Ellsberg. The following June several of the "plumbers" were surprised and captured during a break-in at the headquarters of the Democratic National Committee at the Watergate apartments in Washington, thus setting in motion the stunning series of revelations which led to Nixon's resignation in disgrace in August 1974.

Whereas much of the public and many members of Congress had acquiesed in deception and killing on a large scale in Indochina from 1964 to 1972, in 1973 and 1974 most were unwilling to look the other way while Nixon sought desperately to conceal his involvement in the violation of civil liberties at home. Unchecked government power growing out of the Cold War—visible earlier in the activities of official intelligence agencies and now in the excesses of the "plumbers"—was claiming its most prominent victim.

In fairness, it is important to note that, like Johnson in 1964, Nixon received more than 60 percent of the popular vote in the 1972 election; and that his and Kissinger's imaginative policies toward Russia and China, combined with real progress by October 1972 in winding down the American involvement in Vietnam, contributed to his landslide victory. In Nixon and Kissinger, the leaders in Moscow and Peking found Americans who spoke the understandable language of balance of power and who avoided proclaiming that the United States had the right to rule abroad because of its moral superiority. At a time when conditions within all three nations were favorable for improved East-West relations, Soviet and Chinese leaders discovered practical, hard-nosed American officials with whom they could strike deals.

As both the lengthy Nixon and Kissinger memoirs make clear, American relations with Russia between 1969 and 1972 were extremely complicated. There was an assumption, carried over from the 1963–1968 period, that continued improvement in relations was in the interest of both countries. But there also was a determination on each side that the other would have to pay an adequate price for specific gains in bilateral relations. To the Soviets, for example, America would need to show restraint in Vietnam; to the Americans, Russia would need to help in achieving mutually acceptable settlements in such places as Vietnam and the Middle East. Perhaps because Moscow seemed more anxious than Washington to improve relations, American leaders stuck more consistently—though often unsuccessfully—to their policy of "linkage," the idea that progress in one area depended on progress in others. People living through this period and reading headlines about the ultimate successes in Soviet-American relations had little idea how much posturing and hard negotiating went into the agreements which were finalized in 1971 and 1972.

Although there were Soviet-American agreements on numerous minor issues similar to those negotiated during the Johnson years, the most important agreements involved lessening tensions in Europe, stabilizing the strategic arms race, and increasing Soviet-American trade. In the first area, West German Chancellor Willy Brandt took the lead and the Nixon administration, despite some misgivings, followed. After West Germany formally agreed in August 1970 to recognize the Oder-Neisse line as the permanent border between East Germany and Poland, East-West negotiations proceeded rapidly toward normalization of Western access to, and rights in, West Berlin (completed in April 1971) and the establishment of full "inner-German" relations between East and West Germany (completed in December 1972). The Berlin issue, which earlier had been a barometer of the Cold War atmosphere, finally had been resolved through negotiations.

The Soviet-American strategic arms limitation talks (SALT) proved more difficult for many reasons, not the least of which was the momentum of the arms race itself. Before one new development in missile technology could be fully understood, a second was declared technically feasible and a third, even more lethal, was on the drawing boards.

Another issue was what to include and what to omit from the treaty: should medium-range American missiles deployed in Western Europe and capable of reaching Russia be included, for example, or should the negotiations be limited to long-range missiles? Although the talks began in November 1969, it was not until May 1971 that a breakthrough involving a key compromise by each side was announced. Russia agreed to ignore the thousands of nuclear weapons the United States could deliver from Western Europe and nearby waters, and America granted the Soviets a 3 to 2 edge in the number of ICBMs. The actual SALT I agreements, one setting five-year numerical limits on ICBMs and the other permanent limits on ABMs, were completed and signed in Moscow during Nixon's historic visit—the first by an American president in peacetime—in May 1972.

As in most important international negotiations, success required persistence, an atmosphere of mutual respect, and key concessions by both sides. Over the objections of hawks in the Pentagon and in Congress, the president insisted that the American goal in the nuclear arms race should be "sufficiency" rather than overwhelming superiority. Now that the Soviets had pulled relatively even in strategic arms, it would have been expensive for the U.S. to have tried to maintain a large lead. As Nixon and Kissinger realized, it also would have been self-defeating, for the Soviets could match the United States missile for missile, thus increasing the risk of total annihilation if all-out war between the two nations ever occurred.

Kissinger masterfully orchestrated the negotiations—minimizing bureaucratic delays in Washington, educating the Russians on arms control issues, and at times bypassing the official SALT negotiators in order to deal directly with the Kremlin. Soviet leaders also helped make agreement possible by not insisting on restraining the Americans' technological superiority in such key areas as multiple-warheads and missile-launching submarines and MIRV (multiple independently targeted reentry vehicle) missiles, which, by allowing the U.S. to fire several warheads from one ICBM, offset Russia's numerical advantage. And with the continuing Sino-Soviet split, the Russians had to be prepared to defend themselves, if necessary, against both China and the Western alliance.

The Russians were quite anxious to increase Soviet-American trade, especially in such areas as foodstuffs and high-technology items, which could improve their production of consumer goods. Despite pressure from liberals in Congress and from the business community, Nixon and Kissinger moved slowly in this area. "I do not accept the philosophy that increased trade results in improved political relations . . . ," Nixon told a National Security Council meeting in May 1969. "Better political relations lead to improved trade." As he noted in his memoirs, Kissinger also believed firmly in linking progress on trade to progress in other areas, and he acknowledged that there was dissatisfaction within the State and Commerce departments in regard to this stance.

Because the two top leaders steadfastly maintained their

position, the breakthrough on American trade with Russia occurred only after the SALT treaty and other steps toward détente had been taken at the Moscow summit. That summer the administration permitted the Soviets to begin making large purchases of American grain, and on October 18 a significant trade agreement was signed in which Russia was offered most-favored-nation treatment (that is, the lowest regular tariff rates) and Export-Import Bank loans in exchange for gradual repayment of $722 million in World War II debts. Although this liberalized trade program soon ran into serious roadblocks in Congress, Soviet-American trade grew from $220 million in 1971 to $2.8 billion in 1978. The administration's structure of peace had acquired another important building block.

One of the last agreements signed by Nixon and Brezhnev at the Moscow summit was a declaration on "basic principles" guiding Soviet-American relations. Listed first was their "common determination that in the nuclear age there is no alternative to conducting their mutual relations on the basis of peaceful coexistence," followed by the equally vague agreement to avoid the "development of situations capable of causing a dangerous exacerbation of their relations." Arms limitation, economic and cultural ties, and other constructive goals were mentioned. The Kennedy, Johnson, and Nixon administrations—and their Soviet counterparts—already had proceeded far along this road toward improving relations and ending the Cold War. But even in the euphoria of 1972, one key question remained: Is it possible to maintain the momentum of détente between the two great military and political rivals of modern times?

Although the Moscow summit in May 1972 resulted in numerous specific agreements, the highlight of Nixon's presidency almost certainly was his trip to China three months earlier. Like the trip to Moscow, this dramatic encounter between countries lacking formal diplomatic relations was three years in the making, with the decisive breakthroughs occurring in 1970 and 1971. But whereas the expanded détente with Russia seemed a fairly logical outgrowth of the substantial improvement in Soviet-American relations after 1962, America and China seemed as far apart on the basic issues of Taiwan and American power in Asia when Nixon became president in 1969 as they had been when he became vice-president in 1953. Given the record of two decades of bitter Sino-American hostility, it is not surprising that Nixon felt justified in proclaiming, in a toast during his last evening in Peking, "This was the week that changed the world."

As in Soviet-American relations, there was no straight line toward inevitable rapprochement running from Nixon's inaugural address to his journey to China. Instead, there was much hesitation and uncertainty on both sides in 1969 and 1970. "The new Administration had the general intention of making a fresh start," Kissinger recalled. "But in all candor it had no precise idea how to do this and it had to take account of domestic realities, not the least of which was Nixon's traditional support among the conservative 'China lobby' that had never forgiven Truman and Acheson for allegedly betraying Chiang Kai-shek." The Chinese—still in disarray from the excesses of their "Great Cultural Revolution"—also lacked clear direction in 1969, as when they abruptly canceled meetings with American representatives in Warsaw on February 18, two days before they were scheduled to begin, and unleashed a propaganda attack against the Nixon administration. Throughout 1969 the issue of whether to pursue a moderate or a hard-line policy toward the United States became enmeshed in a power struggle within the Chinese leadership, with the moderate forces led by Chou En-lai generally on the ascendant by the end of the year.

Contributing immeasurably to the possibility of improved relations with America was the durable Sino-Soviet split which, in addition to the usual vitriolic rhetoric, resulted in 1969 in fairly serious military clashes at several points along China's long border with Russia. In this struggle against a recognized superpower, China obviously needed at least diplomatic support. On the other hand, the Nixon administration's bold policies in Indochina—especially the invasion of Cambodia in 1970, which Mao personally denounced—increased the difficulty of maintaining the momentum toward détente. Indeed, until it became clear by late 1970 that the administration definitely was lessening its military involvement in Asia, the prospects for a genuine improvement in Sino-American relations remained in doubt. In a real sense, therefore, the Chinese were playing a linkage game of their own: let America show progress in ending the involvement in Indochina and indicate a willingness to discuss Taiwan, and we will welcome its leaders in Peking.

If Mao and Chou considered improved Sino-American relations to be in China's interest, Nixon and Kissinger agreed for reasons of their own. As Kissinger noted in his memoirs, "Nixon saw in the opening to China a somewhat greater opportunity than I to squeeze the Soviet Union into short-term help on Vietnam; I was more concerned with the policy's impact on the structure of international relations." But both leaders agreed on the basic point "that if relations could be developed with both the Soviet Union and China the triangular relationship would give us a great strategic opportunity for peace." Stated bluntly, America as balancer would be able to play the two communist rivals off against each other. Moreover, improved relations would tend to disarm the many American liberals who had been calling for years for improved relations with China, but who in 1969 and 1970 were concentrating their energies on denouncing Nixon's continuation of the war in Indochina. Finally, an opening to China would help to assuage the American public's deep longing for peace, cast Nixon in a starring role as chief peacemaker, and thus assist in ensuring his reelection in 1972.

Although there were many signals in 1969 and especially in 1970 indicating that both sides would welcome an improvement in relations, perhaps the single most important American move was Nixon's public use of the term "People's Republic of China" twice in October 1970. No previous American president had referred to mainland China by its official name, and Nixon used it both in a press conference and in formally greeting the visiting president of Rumania in late October. Privately, Nixon told President Nicolae Ceausescu that America and China could exchange high-level representatives, and Ceausescu agreed to convey this information to Peking. In addition to the "Rumanian channel," Nixon also used Pakistani President Yahya Khan to convey messages directly to Peking. These initiatives soon bore fruit, for Chou told Yahya on December 9 that Nixon's representative would be welcome in Peking to discuss Taiwan, and Mao told American writer Edgar Snow on December 18 that Nixon himself would be welcome to come. By the following May, Nixon privately had agreed to accept China's formal invitation to visit Peking, and Kissinger was to go there in July to make arrangements for the visit.

Arriving in Peking secretly on July 9, 1971, Kissinger quickly began his talks with Chou, whom Kissinger later described as "one of the two or three most impressive men I have ever met." In their lengthy conversations the two leaders worked on developing mutual confidence and sketching out the two nations' general outlook on world affairs. Wishing to build a positive atmosphere for future negotiations, they avoided wrangling over controversial issues like Taiwan and Vietnam. In fact, the future of Taiwan was discussed only briefly and in generalities. "There is turmoil under the heavens," Chou remarked at one point. "And we have the opportunity to end it." Kissinger remembered being "elated" as his plane left Peking for Pakistan on July 11.

Although many Americans had sensed that something important was brewing when the Chinese invited an American ping-pong team to visit China the previous April, there was still genuine surprise when Nixon went on television on July 15 to announce that he would be visiting the People's Republic "before May 1972" in order to "seek the normalization of relations between the two countries and also to exchange views on questions of concern to the two sides." Expecting an adverse reaction in Russia, Taiwan, South Korea, and Japan, none of which were consulted or informed in advance, Nixon promised that the shift in policy "will not be at the expense of our old friends" and "is not directed against any other nation." Ecstatic that his policy was succeeding, Nixon ignored demonstrators chanting "Get out of Vietnam" as he left the television studios, and proudly introduced Kissinger to startled patrons at a restaurant where the presidential party celebrated the breakthrough on China.

Given the dramatic announcement in July 1971, combined with the mounting international pressures since the early 1960s for Peking's admission to the United Nations as the only lawful government of China, it is not surprising that the new, hastily improvised U.S. proposal that *both* Chinese governments should have seats in the U.N. was not accepted in the General Assembly that fall. When Peking continued to refuse to sit in the U.N. as long as Chiang Kai-shek's government on Taiwan was represented, the General Assembly, despite strenuous U.S. diplomatic efforts, expelled Chiang's regime and admitted the People's Republic by a vote of 76 to 35. While remnants of the once-powerful "China lobby" denounced Nixon's alleged treachery toward Taiwan, most politicians and commentators praised the administration for recognizing realities in Asia, which previous leaders since 1949 had chosen to ignore. Partially reflecting the highly favorable image of China in the media, public opinion polls showed overwhelming support for the president's policies.

Like Khrushchev's visit to America in 1959, Nixon's visit to China in February 1972 was one big media event. A planeload of journalists accompanied American officials to Peking, and the three leading television networks competed with each other to provide the "best" coverage of the visit. In a sense, the most obvious shift in the technology of television paralleled the shift in the Cold War: whereas coverage before 1963 was in stark black-and-white, by the Nixon years most Americans were viewing world affairs in the full spectrum of lifelike color. Even though the negotiations were private, and the networks thus devoted much time to mundane details of life in China and Nixon's visit to the Great Wall, the coverage received high ratings. More than at any other time in his presidency, Nixon came across to the public as a statesman, a sagacious man of peace.

As American officials had warned before the trip, the week of negotiations in Peking involved much hard bargaining and little progress on the key issue separating the two sides, Taiwan. Indeed, the two nations issued separate statements on Taiwan near the end of the meetings. The Chinese insisted that Taiwan was "a province of China," that they had the right to "liberate" it, and that, to normalize relations with Peking, America would have to sever diplomatic relations with Taiwan and remove all of its troops from the island. While officially taking note for the first time of Peking's view that Taiwan was "part of China," the Americans insisted that differences between China and Taiwan had to be resolved peacefully, and they promised vaguely that the United States would remove its troops from Taiwan "as the tension in the area diminishes." In their joint statement, the two nations took the much more positive view that "the normalization of relations between the two countries is not only in the interest of the Chinese and American peoples but also contributes to the relaxation of tension in Asia and the world." In what Nixon considered the most important portion of the joint communiqué, both promised not to "seek hegemony in the Asia Pacific region" and to oppose efforts by other powers (meaning Russia) to do so.

Given agreement on these points, the cordial atmosphere throughout the talks, and lesser agreements in cultural and other areas, leaders on both sides considered the trip a good start toward normalizing Sino-American relations. After some additional progress during the Nixon years, full diplomatic relations were established by new American and Chinese leaders on January 1, 1979.

In achieving their goal of reducing East-West tensions while maintaining a central role for the United States in world affairs, Nixon and Kissinger used what might be called the diplomacy of ambiguity. In contrast to some American leaders earlier in the Cold War, the two statesmen were not interested in specifying which nations were America's friends and enemies. As the president commented in announcing his trip to China: "Any nation can be our friend without being any other nation's enemy." By keeping both traditional allies and adversaries off guard, the administration was able to maintain America's influence in world affairs at a time when its relative military and economic position was declining.

Nixon and Kissinger also realized that considerable ambiguity would be required to improve U.S. relations simultaneously with Russia and China. In dealing with Russia, one does not try to define in advance precisely what "détente" means; nor does one risk the loss of negotiating leverage by giving the impression that the United States is overly anxious to improve relations. In dealing with China, it is wise to work to create a favorable atmosphere by taking small steps and emphasizing common interests, rather than immediately tackling explosive issues like Taiwan. And when the question of Taiwan does arise, agree in principle that Taiwan is part of China but postpone negotiations on details until all affected nations have had time to adjust to the new Sino-American relationship. Recognizing that international relations usually are more analogous to the subtle nuances of personal relationships than to the strict prescriptions of contract law, Nixon, Kissinger, and their Soviet and Chinese counterparts left a record unique in post-1945 great power diplomacy.

Conclusion

An important irony runs through American foreign policy during the 1963–1972 period of the Cold War: at the same time that the United States was working to improve relations with Russia and China, it became deeply involved in a brutal war in Indochina fought ostensibly to prevent the spread of Russian and Chinese influence in Asia. I have advanced the familiar argument that both Johnson and Nixon acted foolishly in sending hundreds of thousands of U.S. troops to fight in Vietnam beginning in 1965 and in keeping them there long after it became apparent to most observers that the United States would not achieve a military victory. Yet the Vietnam War may not have been entirely in vain, for Nixon and Kissinger might not have worked as hard as they did to improve relations with Russia and China if they—and many other Americans as well—had not learned from the Vietnam experience that the United States clearly was overextended in Asia. Indeed, many of their positive initiatives toward both countries resulted partially from their desire to get help in ending the war in such a way as to preserve America's "honor."

A second paradox of this period is that, although it took until 1971 to establish effective bilateral communications with China, American leaders actually felt considerably more comfortable in their new relations with Peking than they did in their long-standing relations with Moscow. Kissinger, for example, referred to the Moscow summit as "more random and jagged" than the one in Peking, and he noted perceptively that "we were geopolitically too competitive with the Soviet Union" for a "common appreciation of the international situation" to emerge. Even though America and Russia had been negotiating seriously in many forums since the mid-1950s, the element of competition between the two superpowers could not be overcome even at the height of Soviet-American détente.

A third paradox involves the nuclear arms race. During these years the United States and Russia negotiated the test ban treaty, the non-proliferation treaty, and the SALT I agreements. Yet the nuclear competition continued, with both sides increasing their arsenals of nuclear warheads and offensive delivery systems and—with the U.S. in the lead—adopting new weapons technology more and more difficult to verify in any future agreement. The arms control talks gave both sides the feeling that they lived in a less dangerous world, and it is true that the talks in themselves lessened East-West tensions. But despite the negotiations, which continued throughout the 1970s, a larger proportion of the American and the Russian people would probably be obliterated if all-out war occurred today than in 1963 or 1972.

One final conclusion about these years is not paradoxical, for it seems as valid in great power relations as it is in personal or group dynamics. As leaders like Rusk, Kissinger, Chou, and Gromyko knew, it takes both hard work and imagination to bring about genuine improvements in great power relations; as in personal relationships, it takes only carelessness and a little posturing to set them back. And, as events since 1972 have shown, even the painstaking achievement of relative détente in which both sides have a stake is no guarantee that two proud, nationalistic superpowers can maintain the upward trend.

CHAPTER FOUR

The Roller-Coaster Years, 1973–1987

In late June 1973, Leonid Brezhnev and other Soviet leaders spent nearly two weeks in the United States, meeting with top American officials and seeking to build upon the achievements of the Moscow summit the previous year. Although there were no new treaties of the magnitude of SALT, Brezhnev and President Nixon did sign an agreement to try to negotiate a treaty in 1974 that would end the nuclear arms race. They also signed agreements in such diverse areas as oceanography, transportation, agriculture, and cultural exchange. Throughout his visit, Brezhnev emphasized the benefits of improved relations, especially in East-West trade and in arms control, and insisted that all problems in Soviet-American relations could be solved as long as both parties did not seek unilateral advantage and were prepared to compromise. In private meetings with Nixon and Kissinger, the Soviet leader expressed deep concern about the situation in the Middle East, implying that a new war would erupt if a peace settlement between Israel and its Arab neighbors was not negotiated quickly. Overall, however, the 1973 summit was quite positive, with both sides affirming their commitment to arms control, increased trade, and other components of détente.

In early October—less than four months later—Egypt and Syria attacked Israeli forces in lands that Israel had occupied six years earlier, thus initiating the fourth major Arab-Israeli war since 1948. Using largely Russian equipment, Egypt and Syria gained the early advantage, but then Israel, aided by massive airlifts of American supplies, fought back and threatened to rout the Arab forces. When Israel ignored U.N. cease-fire resolutions passed on October 22 and 23, Brezhnev sent an urgent letter to the White House on October 24 stating that America and Russia together should send troops to enforce the cease-fire. If the United States refused to act jointly, Brezhnev warned, the Soviets would be forced to "consider . . . taking appropriate steps unilaterally." Viewing this message as an ultimatum, Kissinger quickly convened a special National Security Council meeting that Nixon, preoccupied by his Watergate troubles, did not attend. At this meeting it was decided to issue a DEFCON III (Defense Condition 3) military alert, which is only two steps away from war. Whether this alert altered Russian behavior is not known; but Russian troops were not sent to Egypt, and a cease-fire finally occurred after Kissinger exerted strong and repeated pressure on Israel. The main point here is that Brezhnev's letter and the American response presented a much more somber view of Soviet-American relations than the recent summit; indeed, it was the most serious confrontation since the Cuban missile crisis eleven years before.

The up-and-down effect produced by these two contrasting episodes occurred repeatedly in Soviet-American relations between 1973 and 1987, thus evoking the image of a roller-coaster ride to characterize this era. In fact, given the frequency of leadership changes in both countries during these years—each had four different top leaders and the United States had six different secretaries of state—it might well be viewed as several roller-coaster rides. More than in earlier years, both countries experienced uncertainty and inconsistency in foreign policy; and both possessed less relative power and less inherent respect in their alliance systems than they had in the early post–World War II period. But at least they stayed on the tracks in the most important sense: avoiding the nuclear war between them that could end modern civilization as we know it.

Détente Bogs Down, 1973–1976

President Nixon's overwhelming reelection in November 1972, the Vietnam peace agreement the following January, and the strong commitment to détente within the Soviet leadership boded well for even greater improvements in East-West relations. Those most responsible for the day-to-day operation of foreign affairs in each country—Foreign Minister Andrei Gromyko in Russia and Henry Kissinger in the United States—were capable, experienced diplomats who sought improved relations. Yet, the hopes of leaders in both countries were frustrated as often as they were fulfilled during these four years; and by 1975–1976—or perhaps earlier—Soviet-American relations seemed to be heading slowly but steadily downhill.

Why did this unexpected shift in momentum occur? Why did Soviet-American relations reach a plateau in 1972–1973 and then begin to decline thereafter? A multitude of interrelated factors were involved, but seven seem especially important in understanding why détente bogged down during this period: 1) different understandings of détente among Soviet and American leaders; 2) continuing Soviet-American competition in the Third World; 3) the failure of the SALT process to slow the arms race significantly; 4) the breakdown of the Cold War consensus in U.S. public opinion, combined with failure to achieve a prodétente consensus; 5) a decline in effective presidential leadership coupled with increased congressional assertiveness in foreign policy; 6) the skill of Senator Henry Jackson (Dem., Washington) and other opponents of détente in linking human rights, especially Jewish emigration, with trade issues, thus serving as a focal point for anti-Russian and anti-Kissinger sentiments; and 7) the almost inevitable presence of Soviet-American relations as a major issue in the 1976 election. Thus, although the problems that Soviet-American relations encountered resulted partly from the assumptions and actions of the leaders of both nations and from the generally competitive nature of international relations, internal American attitudes and political practices also were deeply involved in the gradual shift away from détente. As Raymond L. Garthoff has observed in *Detente and Confrontation; American-Soviet Relations from Nixon to Reagan* (1985), "ultimately the fate of efforts to sustain detente . . . in the 1970s foundered on domestic political considerations in the United States as much as on any other factor."

1. Different understandings of détente. A couple entering a marriage with divergent assumptions about how the housework and finances will be handled is headed for trouble and so are two nations with different outlooks that are trying to develop and sustain an improved relationship. Détente continued to be the official policy of both governments until late 1979 because they both sought to reconcile, or at least to live with, their differences. But contrasts in their conceptions of détente harmed relations even during the hopeful years of the early 1970s. By mid-decade, harsh statements to the effect that the other was not "living up to détente" became common in each country.

John Lewis Gaddis has written that Nixon and Kissinger saw détente as "yet another in a long series of attempts to 'contain' the power and influence of the Soviet Union, but one based on a new combination of pressures and inducements that would, if successful, convince the Russians that it was in their own best interests to be 'contained.' " Kissinger viewed détente as involving the need to "manage the emergence of Soviet power"—with the United States (i.e., Kissinger) doing much of the managing. This management would include agreements to limit the nuclear arms race, trade agreements, which American leaders thought the Soviets wanted and needed more than the United States; and restraint in intervening in the Third World, which was meant to apply especially to Soviet behavior.

Some U.S. officials—especially in the State Department—believed that improving Soviet-American relations in such areas as arms control and trade were in America's national interest and, therefore, should not be tied to other issues (such as Soviet behavior in the Third World) in order to try to extract concessions. But Nixon and Kissinger strongly believed in what they called "linkage," and they had the dominant influence in U.S. policy. Thus, while there were many agreements normalizing Soviet-American relations in this period, the administration's conception of détente largely meant using traditional carrot-and-stick diplomacy to influence Soviet foreign policy.

Not surprisingly, Soviet leaders viewed détente differently. They believed that détente had been made possible by the Soviet strategic buildup of the 1960s. As Brezhnev commented in 1975: "Détente became possible because a new correlation of forces in the world arena has been established. Now the leaders of the bourgeois world can no longer seriously count on resolving the historic conflict between capitalism and socialism by force." In contrast to Kissinger, Soviet leaders saw the main task of détente to be the management of America's decline from preeminence in world affairs to a position of relative equality with the USSR. Because of Russia's nuclear strength, America could no longer intimidate the Soviet Union, as it had done during the Cuban missile crisis, nor could it intervene with impunity in the Third World, confident that Russia could not react strongly. Concerned about China's growing nuclear strength, Brezhnev hoped that the United States would join Russia in a de facto alliance against the Chinese. He and Gromyko also warned that a Sino-American military alliance would lead to war.

Soviet leaders took great pride in SALT and other agreements of the early 1970s because they believed that they confirmed Russia's standing as a superpower deserving full equality with the United States in world affairs. Indeed, one of the recurring words in Soviet speeches and writings of the 1970s was "equal"—such as in "equal security" and "equal relations." To the Soviets, it was inappropriate for America to seek to use linkage to extract concessions from a recognized superpower. What Russian leaders did not realize was that, in practice, Nixon and Kissinger—plus the large number of continuing Cold Warriors—were not prepared to grant Russia the complete equality that it considered to be its due.

Finally, the two nations disagreed in their understanding of the likely effects of détente on revolutionary change in the Third World. The Soviets insisted that détente could not halt the movement of history in the direction of socialism, a tenet of Marxist ideology that they believed was confirmed by the experience of the twentieth century. They would not need to "export revolutions" for this inexorable historical process to continue. American leaders, in contrast, saw détente as leading to greater stability and the enhancement of what Kissinger called "American values." In seeking improved relations, neither side was about to change its basic ideology.

2. *Continuing competition in the Third World.* In the Basic Principles Agreement, signed at the Moscow summit in May 1972, Soviet and American leaders pledged to "always exercise restraint in their mutual relations" and to resist the temptation

to "obtain unilateral advantages at the expense of the other
. . ." Like some of the Yalta agreements, these and similar
pledges had two key drawbacks: first, they were too general
and idealistic to be implemented as long as both countries
disagreed sharply on the rights and wrongs of particular conflicts; and, second, they could be quoted in an accusatory fash-
ion by leaders of the two countries against each other and by
opponents of détente against its supporters. Despite the Basic
Principles Agreement and other affirmations of restraint and
cooperation, the Cold War pattern of open or secret aid to
governments or to revolutionary groups continued. From 1973
to 1976, Soviet-American rivalry in the Third World occurred
mainly in the Middle East, in Southeast Asia, and in Africa.

   Even more than before the October 1973 Arab-Israeli war,
the United States was the dominant outside power in the Middle East. America not only supplied large quantities of modern
weapons to four major countries in the region—Israel, Egypt,
Saudi Arabia, and Iran—but also, through Kissinger, played
the leading role in the ongoing peace negotiations between
Israel and its Arab neighbors. Russian leaders objected to their
exclusion from the main developments in a region much closer
to Moscow than to Washington. They also complained that
Kissinger was ignoring the pledges of superpower equality—
which indeed he was. But while Kissinger made some progress
in disengaging hostile armies and in returning some captured
land to the Arabs, no movement was made in the direction
of providing either territory or political rights for the Pales-
tinians. The United States was also unable to prevent an Arab
oil embargo in response to U.S. support for Israel in the war
and a sharp rise in oil prices thereafter that triggered a new
round of inflation at home. In short, although Soviet influence
in the Middle East declined, Kissinger made only modest progress toward a more general Mideast peace and proved unable
to counter the oil producers' new assertiveness.

   In Southeast Asia, America's allies in Indochina finally
lost the war. Receiving some arms and economic assistance
but no direct U.S. military support after January 1973, the

South Vietnamese government fought on alone until Saigon fell to North Vietnamese and Vietcong troops on May 1, 1975. The United States continued heavy bombing in Cambodia for seven months after ending its direct involvement in Vietnam; but Cambodia, too, finally was taken over in April 1975 by a local communist movement allied with China rather than with Russia. Laos, meanwhile, had come under the control of a communist party largely subservient to North Vietnam. As with the "fall of China" a generation before, conservatives argued that the "fall of Indochina" could have been avoided if the U.S. had shown greater resolve. On the other hand, many liberals were quietly pleased that the nation lost a war that, many had concluded, the U.S. should never have entered. As the major ally of North Vietnam, Russia could be viewed as the superpower winner in the conflict. But except for receiving the abandoned U.S. naval base at Camranh Bay, what Russia really acquired was a desperately poor and war-torn country that needed seemingly unlimited amounts of economic and military aid.

The area of greatest Soviet-American tensions in the 1970s, at least from the American viewpoint, was Africa. During the administration of President Gerald Ford (August 1974–January 1977), East-West competition centered in Rhodesia (Zimbabwe) and Angola. Named for the famous British businessman and colonizer, Cecil Rhodes, Rhodesia had long been ruled by its white minority with little interference from the nominal colonial ruler, Britain. In the 1960s, some factions of blacks, who made up well over 90 percent of the population, began to organize to achieve majority rule in the nation they called Zimbabwe. As guerrilla warfare between whites and blacks and tensions among various black liberation groups intensified in the mid-1970s, the United States, Russia, and China all became involved in modest but significant ways. In the early 1970s, the administration had showed little interest in Rhodesia, but in 1976 Kissinger strongly supported Britain's effort to negotiate a transition to majority rule in the country, thereby avoiding serious conflict with either the black majority or with their supporters—the Chinese, the Russians, and other African nations. Skillful British mediation and U.S. support for peaceful change helped blacks and whites to work out the details for elections and a black-led government in the late 1970s.

The situation in Angola proved more difficult to resolve and much more damaging to détente. In contrast to Britain's role in the crisis in Rhodesia, in Angola the colonial power, Portugal, pulled out of the country quickly in 1974 and 1975. The result was a struggle for power among three major political groups: the National Liberation Front of Angola (FNLA), the Popular Movement for the Liberation of Angola (MPLA), and the National Union for the Total Independence of Angola (UNITA). Each of these groups had support in particular tribes, and each sought outside support in order to defeat its rivals and take power. In retrospect, it probably would have been better for Angola if the major outside powers—China, Russia, the United States, South Africa, Zaire, and Cuba—had agreed to stay out of the civil war. But that would have been difficult to negotiate because of the rapidly shifting situation in Angola and because China and Russia and America and Cuba were barely talking to each other, much less working together for common goals.

From the U.S. viewpoint, Angola was damaging to détente because Russia's intervention was more forceful and successful than it had usually been in Third World conflicts. The faction that Russia supported, the MPLA, was largely successful in gaining power in 1975–1976—and international acceptance as the lawful government—whereas Chinese aid to the FNLA and covert U.S. aid to both the FNLA and UNITA proved ineffective. Moreover, the tide turned in MPLA's favor after 250 Cuban military advisers arrived in Angola in June 1975 to instruct MPLA forces. When South Africa sent roughly two thousand troops into Angola in October to assist UNITA, Cuba countered by airlifting fourteen thousand of its troops to assist MPLA. Because South Africa was detested among black Africans for its white supremacist policies and for its colonial occupation of Namibia (old Southwest Africa), the Cuban action was generally viewed by black African governments as necessary to prevent the further spread of South African influence. But because Cuba was closely allied with Russia, without whose aid it would not have been able to intervene in Angola, many Americans saw the use of Cuban troops in Angola as a bold new form of Soviet imperialism and a challenge to America's standing in world affairs. Both the Ford administration and many conservatives were angered when Congress, wary of foreign interventions in the wake of Vietnam and uncomfortable at finding America associated with white-supremacist South Africa, cut off U.S. aid to FNLA and UNITA in early 1976.

Soviet leaders considered their involvement in Angola as being consistent with détente. They insisted that they had as much right to assist "progressive forces" in the Third World as China, America, and South Africa had to help their factions. They also believed that they had been shunted aside in the Middle East and that letting the Chinese and Americans push them aside in Africa would be a serious blow to their prestige and to their status as a superpower. Still viewing conflicts in the Third World largely in East-West terms, most Americans did not realize that Russia was intervening in Angola in large part to defeat its bitter rival, China. In criticizing Russia's use of Cuban troops in Angola, Americans also did not note similarities with their own use of South Korean and other Asian troops in Vietnam that the Soviets might equally view as proxies. Regardless of the merit of Soviet defenses of their own and Cuba's behavior in Angola, however, the fact remained that it proved helpful to antidétente forces in the United States. It also led the Ford administration to abandon discreet talks with Cuba, begun in 1974, which might have led to a substantial détente in America's mini–Cold War with that country.

3. *The continuing arms race despite SALT.* Like the Soviet-American rivalry in the Third World, the continuing competition in strategic arms helped to undermine détente in the

1970s. In theory, the 1972 agreements should have been able to end the nuclear arms race because (*a*) the antiballistic missile treaty sharply and permanently curtailed defensive systems, and (*b*) with neither side able to defend itself against a nuclear attack by the other, it should have been possible to freeze the number of offensive arms held by each side and eventually reduce them to a level sufficient to ensure mutual deterrence. Such, indeed, was to have been the goal of SALT II.

Why were the two sides not able to follow up their comprehensive agreement virtually abolishing defensive systems with an agreement effectively to limit offensive systems, thus bringing the Soviet-American nuclear arms race to an end and, in the process, easing the world's anxiety over the possibility of nuclear war and setting an example for other actual or potential nuclear weapons powers? Why, in short, did the nuclear arms race continue virtually unabated?

In retrospect, it appears that the main reason was that the political will to end the arms race was lacking in both countries. Ending the offensive arms race would have required a confrontation by Nixon with the Pentagon, which was used to "staying ahead" of the Soviets technologically by ordering expensive new weapons systems from defense contractors, and a confrontation by Brezhnev with his defense ministry, which was accustomed to getting a large share of the budget for its contractors in order to "catch up" with the Americans. These confrontations did not occur and SALT I and subsequent agreements, instead of limiting offensive arms significantly, largely ratified what each side was already planning to do to "modernize" its strategic forces. For each side, this meant improving the accuracy of its missiles (thus seeking the ability to launch a preemptive "first strike" to destroy the other side's ability to retaliate) and, equally important, putting multiple independently targetable reentry vehicles (MIRVs) on existing and new missiles, so that each missile now could carry several warheads instead of just one. Thus, although the numbers of land- and sea-based missiles and long-range bombers on each

side were limited to 2,400 at a meeting between Presidents
Ford and Brezhnev at Vladivostok, USSR, in November 1974,
the number of warheads was not limited. By the time SALT I
expired in 1977, the United States had roughly 8,500 warheads,
compared to 5,700 in 1972. The Soviets had increased their
warheads from 2,500 to 4,000, and, like the United States, had
improved the accuracy of their delivery systems, thus increasing the threat to America's land-based missiles in the event of
a preemptive attack.

The failure to make more progress in ending the arms race
was disappointing to Nixon and Kissinger. Both were proud
that SALT I established the goal of limiting competition in
strategic weapons; both regretted that more was not accom-
plished before they left office. Kissinger believed that liberals
did not understand the need for a strong defense while new
limits were being negotiated, but he also chastised conservatives for failing to realize that arms control agreements could
enhance U.S. security in the nuclear age. "One of the questions
we have to ask ourselves as a country is what in the name of
God is strategic superiority?" Kissinger commented in 1974.
"What is the significance of it politically, militarily, opera-
tionally, at these levels of numbers? What do you do with it?"
Nixon's remarks to Secretary of Defense James Schlesinger
that same year struck a similar note: "Many of my friends are
horrified at our even talking to the Soviet Union. But are we
going to leave the world running away with an arms race, or
will we get a handle on it?"

4. The lack of consensus in American public opinion. The
1970s saw the greatest ferment and debate of the goals of U.S.
foreign policy—and the appropriate means to achieve them—
since the isolationist versus internationalist confrontation before Pearl Harbor. The belief in an activist, anti-communist
foreign policy had been dominant from about 1947 until the
mid-1960s. But the Vietnam War, together with Nixon's initiatives to improve relations with Russia and China, shattered
the Cold War consensus and left a multitude of opinions about
America's proper role in world affairs. The diversity of atti-

tudes made it difficult for the administration to win broad public and congressional support for specific policies. Although public opinion polls showed that most Americans supported détente, many remained instinctively anti-communist and suspicious of Russia.

The ending of the Cold War consensus was most noticeable among the more knowledgeable and politically active segment of the population. Earlier, this broad grouping had been overwhelmingly supportive of Cold War policies; but by the late 1960s it had split into conservative internationalists on the one side and liberal internationalists on the other. Conservative internationalists tended to remain strongly anti-communist, anti-Russian, promilitary, and in favor of CIA and limited military interventions in the Third World to combat leftist movements. Liberal internationalists favored détente with Russia, arms control, lower defense budgets, much less military and CIA involvement in the Third World, support for human rights instead of right-wing dictators, and international cooperation in addressing such problems as economic development and environmental protection.

In Congress, the perspectives of conservative internationalists such as Senators Jackson and Strom Thurmond (Rep., South Carolina) and liberal internationalists such as Senators Edward Kennedy (Dem., Massachusetts) and Charles Mathias (Rep., Maryland) were so different that the Nixon, Ford, and Carter administrations could not expect unity or consistency in congressional votes on foreign policy. Similarly, after Vietnam the liberal *New York Times* and the conservative *Wall Street Journal* seldom agreed editorially on world affairs. Like most politically active people, both liberal and conservative internationalists had their share of inconsistencies: for example, liberals wanted strong U.S. support for human rights while deploring America's tendency to intervene in other nations' internal affairs, whereas conservatives sought increased budgets for defense and intelligence while cutting the cost of government and lowering taxes.

While the more politically active were dividing sharply in

their views, the roughly one-half of the public who were less interested in and knowledgeable about world affairs tended to be suspicious of government—especially after Vietnam and Watergate—and of foreigners. Basically, as public opinion analyst William Schneider has pointed out, they favored both peace and military strength. They wanted better relations with the Russians but remained distrustful of them. They thought that the United States should stay out of foreign quarrels; yet they were sensitive to slights to America's pride. Because their views were volatile and not based on either a conservative or a liberal ideology, they could provide the swing votes in elections, going for liberal Democrats in one election and conservative Republicans in another.

In short, the Cold War consensus was not replaced by a new one, either in elite or in mass opinion. Neither prodétente nor antidétente forces dominated public opinion or Congress during the 1970s or 1980s, and presidents had to try to appeal to both conservative and liberal strands of thought, often at the same time. As Nixon and his successors learned, the climate of opinion did not facilitate a consistent, stable policy either toward the Soviet Union or toward the often baffling Third World, seen by some in purely Cold War terms and by others as having a wide range of essentially local problems with the need for peace and development as the one unifying theme.

5. *The decline in presidential leadership in foreign policy.* One of the central tenets of the Cold War consensus had been that the country should look to the president for leadership in foreign affairs, especially in standing up to communism. In the 1950s and 1960s, America's Vietnam policy had embodied this principle: Congress dutifully voted billions of dollars in aid for noncommunist Indochina, looked the other way while the CIA undertook extensive operations in the region, and then voted the money for Johnson's and Nixon's expensive war there. In the late 1960s and 1970s, however, there was a barrage of revelations about dubious presidential actions and cover-ups of illegal activities. In the second volume of his memoirs,

Years of Upheaval (1982), Kissinger blamed the new congressional assertiveness in foreign policy, and the resulting decline in presidential authority, largely on Watergate. But it was not just Watergate: it was the cover-up of the My Lai massacre; the cover-up and lying to Congress (which Kissinger participated in) about the bombing of Cambodia; news reports, which turned out to be accurate, about the participation of the CIA and U.S. companies in efforts to overthrow the elected government of Chile; and the growing sense that Nixon's and Kissinger's secrecy, their tendency to bypass the State Department and other officials in making policy, and their general disregard for truth and morality were inconsistent with American ideals and thus required increased congressional supervision of foreign affairs.

The ending of the Cold War consensus in itself increased the need for greater give-and-take between the executive and Congress. But the actions of Nixon and Kissinger in Cambodia and elsewhere during their first term, when these actions came to light after 1972, prompted congressional demands for a sharply increased role in foreign affairs. Applied to Soviet-American relations, the new mood on Capitol Hill meant that any administration proposal would be subject to intense scrutiny and that the Nixon-Kissinger conception of détente would not necessarily be endorsed by a newly skeptical Congress.

6. *Senator Jackson leads the congressional assault on détente.* In 1919–1920, a Republican senator from Massachusetts, Henry Cabot Lodge, orchestrated the forces that defeated President Wilson on the issue of U.S. entry into the League of Nations. In 1973–1975, a Democratic senator from Washington, Henry Jackson, played a similar role in undermining détente with the Soviet Union. Like Lodge, Jackson had served in the Senate for many years at the time of his challenge to administration policy; he was the second-ranking member of the Senate Armed Services Committee, which oversees the Pentagon's budget. A skillful legislator, he knew how to make things happen in Congress; he also had close ties to the Pentagon, defense contractors, organized labor, and the Jewish

community. A conservative internationalist with presidential ambitions, Jackson detested the Soviet Union and believed that it should be approached from a position of military strength and not through trade, arms control, or other components of détente. Kissinger remembered Jackson as a "fierce negotiator" and a "master psychological warrior," and he commented that a meeting with Jackson in March 1974 was "the beginning of a dialogue that made me long for the relative tranquillity of the Middle East."

Jackson's greatest success in undermining détente came in his persistent assault on Soviet-American trade. Jackson knew that increased trade was an important component of détente to the Soviets, who wanted access to U.S. technology and credit to improve their economy. Jackson also knew that, in order to defeat the administration on this issue, he would need the votes of some liberals, both because liberals held the balance of power in Congress and because some conservatives would support the increased trade favored by most U.S. business groups. Accordingly, Jackson embraced the idea of linking congressional support for equality in trade—symbolized by the granting of most-favored-nation tariff status to Russia—to Soviet concessions on Jewish emigration, a concept embodied in the Jackson-Vanik amendment to the trade bill that worked its way through Congress in 1973-1974. Despite business opposition, some conservatives voted for Jackson-Vanik because, like Jackson, they disliked both détente and the Soviet Union; and many liberals voted for it because they deplored anti-Semitism in Russia and considered freedom to emigrate to be a basic human right.

Both the administration and Soviet leaders strongly opposed Jackson-Vanik and other efforts to limit trade. Nixon and Kissinger supported increased Jewish emigration and, in general, more Soviet respect for human rights. But they argued that these goals were more likely to be achieved through quiet diplomacy and tacit understandings than through direct congressional pressure. They also thought that U.S. leaders should be cautious about seeking to change the other super-

power's domestic policies and that linkage should be applied
to Russia's international behavior, not to its internal affairs.
For their part, Soviet leaders had already begun to permit
increased Jewish emigration, but they denounced the idea of
quotas imposed by Congress as meddling in their domestic
affairs. When Congress finally passed a trade bill in December
1974, which included the Jackson-Vanik Amendment and set
a limit of $300 million on U.S. credits to Russia without
congressional approval, the Soviets informed the United States
that they would not implement the provisions of the 1972 trade
agreement. And, as Kissinger had predicted, they also cut back
sharply on Jewish emigration. "I think détente has had a set-
back," Kissinger commented.

Aided by Richard Perle, a hard-working member of his
staff, Jackson also worked persistently to undermine public
and congressional support for arms control agreements. He
argued in 1972 that SALT I gave the Soviets the advantage
and got an amendment through the Senate stating that all
future treaties would have to give the United States numerical
equality in strategic launchers. When Kissinger and Ford gained
Soviet acceptance of that principle in the Vladivostok agreement in 1974, Jackson and Perle denounced the agreement
because (a) the numbers were too high and (b) the Soviets had
more heavy missiles than the United States. In fact, the United
States had chosen not to build heavy missiles, though it would
be free to do so under the agreement. Moreover, Vladivostok
gave the United States the possibility of continued strategic
superiority—assuming that that concept had any meaning at
the current levels of destructive potential—because U.S. forward-based systems (bombers and missiles in Europe and the
Mediterranean) were not counted as part of the 2,400 limit,
whereas the Soviets had no similar forward-based systems.

Jackson and his allies in the Pentagon and in the press
were not interested in an evenhanded analysis of the strategic
balance. They wanted to push ahead with new U.S. weapons
systems and saw the SALT process as undermining support
for defense expenditures. Assisting them were the momentum

of new technology, which now made it possible for the United States to deploy cruise missiles (low-flying missiles that could elude Soviet radar) that, because of their small size, would be difficult to verify and hence to include as part of arms control agreements. The Soviets also had new weapons, including the so-called Backfire bomber. Also assisting opponents of arms control was the public's continuing ignorance of the details of the strategic balance, which permitted conservatives to argue (as the liberal Kennedy had done in 1960) that the United States was falling behind Russia and the SALT process had given the Soviets the advantage. The fact that the two nations' force structures were very different, with the United States having most of its nuclear warheads on submarines and bombers while the Soviets had most of theirs on land-based missiles, also made comparisons difficult. Finally, the fact that both sides were modernizing their forces showed that SALT had not slowed the offensive arms race significantly. But instead of urging new agreements with qualitative as well as quantitative restrictions, conservatives sought to cast doubt on the entire SALT process. This combination of factors, plus fear that the Pentagon and Congress would not support a treaty involving concessions by both sides, made it impossible for Kissinger to conclude a SALT II agreement in early 1976. In a real sense, therefore, Jackson had won at least a partial victory on arms control that accompanied his success in restricting trade.

    7. Détente as an issue in the election of 1976. Nineteen seventy-six was the year of the outsider in American politics. There were plenty of experienced insiders who wanted to be elected president that year—President Ford for the Republicans and Senator Jackson and others for the Democrats—but many of the votes and headlines went to two men with no experience in Washington: an actor and former California governor, Ronald Reagan, for the Republicans, and a peanut farmer and former Georgia governor, Jimmy Carter, for the Democrats. The electorate seemed to be looking for new faces unassociated with either the Vietnam War or Watergate. Reagan opposed détente and Carter appeared to support it while criticizing its implementation; both cast doubt on the wisdom of the approach by their sharp attacks on Ford and Kissinger.

While Carter moved steadily toward the Democratic nomination with his good political organization and his general calls for morality in public life, Ford was facing the toughest fight for the nomination of any incumbent president in this century. An effective speaker who could warm the hearts of conservative audiences, Reagan found that Ford was most vulnerable among Republican voters on foreign policy issues, especially those involving the alleged weakness of the administration on Soviet-American relations and on defense. So Reagan went on the attack. "Let us not be satisfied with a foreign policy whose principle accomplishment seems to be our acquisition of the right to sell Pepsi-Cola in Siberia," Reagan told cheering students in New Hampshire. "Under Kissinger and Ford, this nation has become Number Two in a world where it is dangerous—if not fatal—to be second best," he stated in Florida, and continued, "There is little doubt in my mind that the Soviet Union will not stop taking advantage of détente until it sees that the American people have elected a new President and appointed a new Secretary of State." In reply, Ford defended his foreign policy and accused Reagan of oversimplifying reality; but he also announced that he was dropping *détente* from his vocabulary.

The race turned out to be very close: Ford won most of the primaries in the Northeast and Midwest, but Reagan had the upper hand in the South and West. In late July, Ford had a slight lead in delegates, but the undecided delegates held the balance of power. At the Republican national convention in August, Ford won by the slim margin of 1,187 to 1,070. But he had to accept a platform that, on foreign policy issues, read like some of Reagan's speeches: "In pursuing détente we must not grant unilateral favors with only the hope of getting future favors in return."

Having barely escaped becoming the first sitting president in this century to be denied the nomination of his party, Ford now faced an uphill struggle against Carter. Although the president was able to close the gap in public opinion polls as the campaign progressed, Carter possessed the advantage that had helped Reagan: he could remain on the offensive, whereas Ford had to defend his policies. And Carter did not have to be consistent. He could accuse Ford of giving away too much to the Russians while at the same time he could say that Ford had not tried hard enough to get a new SALT agreement. Still, Ford might have won a narrow victory if he had not made the enormous error, during the second televised debate, of insisting that there was "no Soviet domination of Eastern Europe." This was a statement certain to anger Americans of East European descent and to renew doubts about Ford's intelligence.

Carter won the election with roughly 50 percent of the popular vote to 48 percent for Ford. But during the campaign, neither of the candidates had offered much guidance for the future of Soviet-American relations. As in many election years, there was much politics—but little substance—in U.S. foreign policy in 1976. Détente clearly was on hold, but military technology and the size of the arsenals on both sides were moving forward.

Détente Plus Confrontation, 1977–1980

As a statesman, Jimmy Carter is remembered largely for his achievements outside the area of Soviet-American relations. He is especially known for the Panama Canal treaties of 1977, which showed that politically charged issues can be resolved through negotiations, and for the Camp David accords of 1978, which produced peace between Egypt and Israel. His administration also established full diplomatic relations with the People's Republic of China, negotiated skillfully for a comprehensive treaty to update the law of the seas, and worked hard to improve the human rights situation in many countries and to prevent the spread of nuclear weapons to nations that did not already possess them. These and other efforts to create a more peaceful and just world order may well raise Carter's standing in history.

Yet Carter is unlikely to be praised for his overall handling of Soviet-American relations. His vision was lofty: he said in his inaugural address that, at the end of his presidency, "I would hope that the nations of the world might say that we had built a lasting peace, based not on weapons of war but on international policies which reflect our own most precious values." He also promised that his administration would "move this year a step toward our ultimate goal—the elimination of all nuclear weapons from this earth." Neither the goal for the end of 1977 nor the one for the close of his presidency came close to being achieved. Instead, Soviet-American relations under Carter started off poorly in 1977, recovered just enough to permit the signing of the SALT II treaty in June 1979, and then shifted to bitter hostility when the Soviet Union invaded Afghanistan six months later.

Although Carter alone did not end détente—Soviet actions and by the growing influence of Cold Warriors at home played their part—the president was so inconsistent in his policies and so inept in his political leadership that he also certainly contributed to the downturn in relations from 1977 through 1980. Lacking a clear sense of what he most wanted to achieve and how to achieve it, Carter zigzagged and waffled while losing support both at home and abroad. The president's domestic approval rating in the Gallup poll stood at 67 percent in July 1977, 39 percent in July 1978, 29 percent in July 1979, and 21 percent (an all-time low for the post–1945 presidency) in July 1980. In England, long America's closest ally, 62 percent of respondents in a 1979 poll doubted "the ability of the United States to deal wisely with present world problems."

The difficulties in Soviet-American relations during Carter's first year began, before the inauguration, with his selection of Cyrus Vance to be his secretary of state and Zbigniew Brzezinski to be his national security adviser. Vance, a mild-mannered, modest man who avoided the spotlight, had served effectively in the Democratic administrations of the 1960s. Vance believed that difficulties in Soviet-American relations could be worked out on a case-by-case basis and that most of the problems in the Third World had largely local roots and should not be blamed on the Soviet Union. A liberal internationalist, Vance also opposed linkage, especially on arms control, which he considered to be clearly in the national interest of both nations.

In many ways, Brzezinski was the opposite of Vance. Called by reporters the "Polish Kissinger," Brzezinski in fact had several similarities to his famous predecessor. Both were immigrants (Kissinger from Germany, Brzezinski from Poland) who still spoke with accents; both were respected political scientists at Ivy League universities; and both were highly ambitious men who loved to talk with reporters to seek the limelight. But Brzezinski differed from Kissinger in being instinctively anti-Soviet and in finding a Russian hand in almost every disturbance in the Third World. A conservative internationalist whose views on Soviet-American relations had changed little since the 1950s, Brzezinski also lacked Kissinger's sense of grand strategy. Elizabeth Drew wrote in 1978: "Of all the many people I have discussed the subject of Brzezinski with, hardly any have used the word 'thoughtful.' "

In his memoirs, Carter wrote that he had been warned of some of Brzezinski's character traits—his ambition, aggressiveness, and the possibility that "he might not be adequately deferential to a secretary of state"—before he appointed him. But Carter liked Brzezinski as a person and respected his intellect, and he thought that he could permit Brzezinski and Vance to state different opinions because "the final decisions on basic foreign policy would be made by me in the Oval Office." In fact, however, Brzezinski repeatedly sought to overrule the State Department and to win Carter's support for his ideas or, as in the case of China policy, to seize control of decision making. Moreover, the two men's advice often was incompatible. Yet Carter, with his lack of experience in foreign affairs, often did little more than try to split the difference between them, thus contributing greatly to the inconsistency and incoherence in U.S. policy during these years. Finally, the persistent leaking of conflicting viewpoints to the media by Brzezinski and his staff and by the State Department added to the perception of an administration in disarray.

The incoherence in policy toward the Soviet Union was evident during the administration's first few months in office. The president wanted to carry out his campaign pledge by making human rights a new pillar of U.S. foreign policy. He also wanted to move forward rapidly to achieve a new arms control agreement to replace SALT I, which was to expire in October 1977. With the euphoria that accompanied his becoming president, Carter seemed unconcerned that Soviet leaders would be angered by his stance on human rights; he also brushed aside warnings that they would reject outright his new approach to arms control. From their memoirs, it seems clear that Vance largely disagreed with Carter's confrontational approach during his first few weeks in office, whereas Brzezinski welcomed it.

On human rights, Carter, shortly after his election in November, had sent a telegram of support to Soviet dissident Vladimir Slepak. Carter then instructed Vance to meet in December with an exiled dissident, Andrei Amalrik; shortly after Carter's inauguration, the State Department praised another leading dissident, Andrei Sakharov, and Carter sent a letter of support to Sakharov in mid-February. On March 1, Carter and Vice-President Walter Mondale visited with exiled dissident Vladimir Bukovsky at the White House. In a letter to Carter dated February 25, 1977, Brezhnev denounced the president's correspondence with Sakharov, "a renegade who proclaimed himself an enemy of the Soviet state," and insisted that he would not "allow interference in our internal affairs, whatever pseudo-humanitarian slogans are used to present it."

With the atmosphere thus poisoned, Carter decided to send Vance and chief arms negotiator Paul Warnke to Moscow in late March with a proposal for deep cuts in offensive weapons. Brezhnev and Gromyko gave the two envoys an icy reception and publicly ridiculed their proposal for deep cuts. Because these cuts would affect Soviet land-based missiles significantly while requiring few changes in the U.S. force structure and because the Soviets had insisted that negotiations should proceed along the lines outlined previously at Vladivostok and pursued thereafter by Kissinger and Gromyko, it is remarkable that Carter thought that he had any chance of getting his proposal accepted. It also appears that Carter did not think through either the negative impression a public defeat on this issue would make at home or the effects of his proposal on Soviet attitudes toward him. In regard to the latter, a Soviet official wrote later that this initiative "confirmed the impression in Moscow that Carter was not serious" about arms control.

From here it was a long, slow ride back up the rollercoaster until SALT II was finally signed more than two years later. Carter wanted to have a summit meeting to exchange views with Brezhnev in 1977, but the Soviet leader refused to meet until SALT II was ready for their signatures. Meanwhile Carter gave the impression of inconsistency in his defense policies. He supported some weapons programs that the conservatives wanted—cruise missiles, a counterforce capability for the land-based Minuteman III, and the Trident submarine—but angered them when he canceled two other potential weapons—the B-1 bomber and the neutron (enhanced radiation) bomb, which would kill people while doing less damage to property than other nuclear weapons. Liberals were upset because defense spending was increasing, despite Carter's campaign pledge to cut it, but conservatives did not think that it was growing rapidly enough and gave Carter no credit for his strategic modernization programs.

In addition to human rights and arms control, two other major issues harmed Soviet-American relations and stirred disputes within the administration between 1977 and early 1979. The first of these was the continuing superpower rivalry in Africa, now centered in the so-called Horn of Africa, an area in the northeast corner of the continent close to the stra-

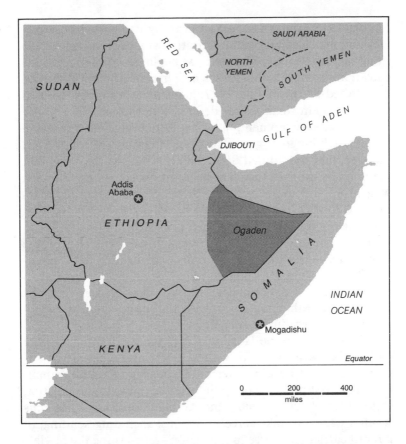

tegic Middle East. In this poor and ethnically divided region, the U.S. had provided Ethiopia with military and economic aid since 1953 and Russia had supplied arms to Somalia beginning in 1963, receiving a naval base on the Somali coast in return. Somali leaders wanted to annex the Ogaden region of Ethiopia, a sparsely populated, largely desert area inhabited mainly by ethnic Somalis. When a Marxist coup and resulting civil war occurred in Ethiopia in 1974, Somali ambitions to seize the Ogaden increased. American aid to Ethiopia continued after the coup, but relations became strained, and in December 1976 Ethiopia signed an arms agreement with the Soviet Union. The Carter administration stopped military aid to Ethiopia the following May, and, when Soviet-Somali relations cooled in response to Moscow's new friendship with Ethiopia, the United States in July 1977 "agreed in principle" to help Somalia obtain weapons for defensive purposes.

At that very moment, however, Somali troops were in the Ogaden helping local guerrillas to oust Ethiopian troops from the area, and the United States did not deliver the arms that the Somalis thought they had been promised. As the Somalis won more and more territory, Soviet-Somali relations deteriorated further, with a complete break occurring in November. The Soviets and Cubans then provided major support to Ethiopia: roughly $1 billion in Russian weapons and twelve to seventeen thousand Cuban troops were airlifted to the country. Between January and March 1978, an Ethiopian-Cuban offensive routed the Somalis from the Ogaden and returned the region to Ethiopian control. At that point the war ended, and the crisis gradually subsided.

The events in the Horn of Africa ignited a bitter dispute within the Carter administration. Brzezinski viewed the situation largely in East-West terms. He believed that the Somali-Ethiopian war posed "a potentially grave threat to our position in the Middle East, notably the Arabian peninsula." He thus wanted Carter to take forceful actions, including sending an aircraft carrier task force to the region and warning the Soviets and Cubans that their actions were causing a serious crisis in Soviet-American relations that could prevent progress on other issues such as arms control. Vance and others in the State Department, however, saw the situation as essentially a local conflict. They believed that the United States should not send arms to Somalia as long as Somali troops were inside Ethiopian territory and that the United States "should continue to work with our European allies and the African nations to bring about a negotiated solution of the broader regional issues." In short, so long as Ethiopian and Cuban troops did not invade Somalia,

America should limit its involvement and not attempt to link the situation to other East-West issues.

In this conflict within the administration, Secretary of Defense Harold Brown sided with Vance, and so largely did President Carter. But Brzezinski still made his influence felt. He leaked his views to the press repeatedly, and he also was "very gratified" when Carter spoke forcefully on the issue in a meeting with a member of the Soviet politburo in January 1978. And when Gromyko proposed a "joint U.S.-Soviet mediation effort," Brzezinski helped to insure that Carter rejected it. Finally, having lost the battle for a policy of linkage within the administration, Brzezinski went public on March 1 with the statement that "linkages may be imposed by unwarranted exploitation of local conflict for larger international purposes." Vance, who believed that a successful outcome of the conflict in the Horn was being achieved, was furious. He responded on the next day that there was "no linkage" between events in the Horn and SALT. But the damage had been done: opponents of détente such as Jackson and Paul Nitze were almost certain to quote Brzezinski in their effort to defeat a SALT II treaty.

Although Brzezinski lost out on overall policy toward the Horn of Africa, he succeeded in setting the direction of U.S. policy toward China from 1978 onward. The Carter administration was united in wanting to achieve normal diplomatic relations with mainland China. But Vance and Brzezinski disagreed on whether the major U.S. objective in normalizing relations was (a) to continue the triangular relationship established by Kissinger, with America as the evenhanded balancer between Russia and China, or (b) to develop a de facto alliance with China against Russia. Vance argued vigorously for the first viewpoint, while Brzezinski worked steadily for the second. Carter does not appear to have recognized how much he was leaning toward Brzezinski's view; but in sending him to Peking in May 1978 (against Vance's strongly stated wishes) and in subsequent actions, the president clearly was "playing the China card" against Russia.

During his trip to Peking, Brzezinski did everything he could to please the Chinese leaders. He told them that America accepted their conditions for normalization; he shared sensitive military information with them; and he stressed repeatedly the evil nature of the Soviet Union and the threat that "the polar bear" posed to peace. His toasts at the formal dinners were almost as anti-Soviet as those of the Chinese. At one dinner he stated that "the United States recognized and shared China's resolve to 'resist the efforts of any nation which seeks to establish global or regional hegemony' "—hegemony being a code word in the standard Chinese denunciation of Russia. Upon his return, Brzezinski told a *New York Times* reporter that the trip was intended to "underline the long-term strategic nature of the United States' relationship to China."

While Carter was pleased with the progress that Brzezinski had made toward normalization, Soviet leaders were deeply concerned. An editorial in *Pravda* on May 30, 1978, stated that Brzezinski "stands before the world as an enemy of détente." *Pravda* also blamed China, stating on June 17 that "Soviet-American confrontation . . . is the cherished dream of Peking." On the whole, U.S. officials were not displeased by the Kremlin's anger and concern: perhaps it would make Soviet leaders more anxious to conclude the SALT negotiations and more inclined to show restraint in the Third World.

Secret Sino-American negotiations proceeded during the summer and fall, and on December 15, 1978, both nations announced that full diplomatic relations would be established on January 1, 1979, followed by a visit by Vice Premier Deng Xiaoping to Washington at the end of the month. Deng used the occasion, and the heavy media coverage it received, to denounce the Soviet Union. Despite Vance's appeal for even-handedness in dealing with Russia and China, Carter agreed to include "hegemony" in the joint communiqué issued at the end of the visit. Deng was playing the American card—his desire for a Sino-American alliance against Russia—at least as effectively as Brzezinski had played the China card in Peking the previous summer.

The SALT II agreement, signed by Carter and Brezhnev in Vienna on June 18, 1979, was the high point (if indeed there was one) of Soviet-American relations during the Carter years. As in 1972, when Brezhnev went ahead with the summit despite the U.S. mining of Haiphong, the Soviet leaders signed the SALT II treaty despite all the recent U.S. actions that, in their view, were undermining détente. But this time the Washington administration, with little public or congressional enthusiasm for the treaty, was unable to persuade the Senate to consent to its ratification. Indeed, the signing of SALT II by an aging, sickly general secretary and an unpopular president did little if anything to slow the downward slide in Soviet-American relations.

The treaty itself was too detailed and too technical to be understood fully by the average citizen or, for that matter, by the average senator. Essentially, however, it limited each side to a total of 2,400 strategic launch vehicles until the end of 1981, and to 2,250 from then until the treaty expired at the end of 1985. Limits also were put on the number of MIRVed land-based missiles (820), on the total number of MIRVed land-based and submarine launched missiles (1,200), and on the total number of these MIRVed missiles and heavy bombers equipped with long-range cruise missiles (1,320). The Soviet Union still had the advantage in total throw weight and in the number of land-based missiles, but the United States led in the number of weapons, submarine-based weapons, cruise missiles, and the forward-based systems that remained outside SALT. The treaty permitted one new land-based missile for each side. As in previous arms control negotiations, SALT II basically let each side do what it was planning to do anyway. But at least it put limits—admittedly very high ones—on the nuclear arms race, and it called for further negotiations to achieve significant cuts in the arsenals on both sides.

Partly in order to try to convince conservative senators that it was tough on defense, the Carter administration urged Congress to approve funds for the deployment of a new land-based missile, the MX, at the same time that it submitted the

SALT treaty for the Senate's approval. It also proceeded, in conjunction with its NATO allies, to move toward the deployment of highly accurate Pershing II and cruise missiles in Western Europe to counter Russia's new intermediate-range missiles, the SS-20s. The new U.S. deployments would not be made if Russia could be persuaded to remove its SS-20s—or if the growing peace movement in several NATO countries could stop them.

It seems unlikely that SALT II would have passed the Senate even without the Soviet invasion of Afghanistan in late December 1979. Carter's political standing was too low, Soviet-American relations were too strained, and conservatives were too opposed to the entire concept of détente (which arms control had come to symbolize) for the administration to muster anywhere near the two-thirds vote required to win Senate consent to ratification. If the same treaty had been negotiated in 1977, when Carter was at the height of his popularity, it might well have passed. But by June 1979, the next presidential campaign was approaching, and most Republicans were not about to ratify an arms control agreement that might help an unpopular president win reelection. Most liberals probably would have voted for it, though many were disappointed that it did not do enough to end the strategic arms race. Thus SALT II remained unratified, widely denounced by conservatives and given lukewarm support at best by liberals. Yet, ironically, it was largely observed by both governments even after it expired in 1985, thus suggesting that it was more balanced and practical—or at least more in tune with the realities of Soviet-American relations and the wishes of defense establishments on both sides—than critics at the time acknowledged.

If the signing of SALT II can be considered a small step upward in Soviet-American relations, the Soviet invasion of Afghanistan in December 1979 created the biggest decline since the Cuban missile crisis or even since the Korean War. The invasion and the U.S. response, Raymond Garthoff has observed, "marked a watershed in American-Soviet relations, sharply dividing the previous decade of détente (admittedly, faltering badly by that time) from the ensuing years of containment and confrontation." Why did Russia make this move, which was almost certain to be viewed with alarm in the West as well as in the Middle East? And why did the Carter administration make a hard-line response to Soviet intervention in a country on Russia's southern border?

As with most great power interventions in small countries, the Soviets said that their sending of troops to Afghanistan was a defensive move. They long had had interests there, but these grew sharply after an April 1978 coup that brought the Marxist People's Democratic Party of Afghanistan (P.D.P.A.) to power in the capital, Kabul. When it tried to bring about land reform and other social changes in the conservative Moslem countryside, armed resistance developed. And when the P.D.P.A. chose in early 1979 to try to crush this resistance by air raids and other military tactics, the Russian-backed government rapidly lost much of its small popular support. Brezhnev explained in June 1980 that Russia "had no choice but to send troops" in order to "preserve the gains of the April revolution." Brezhnev and other Soviet spokesmen also argued, with some justification, that their bitter enemy China, the United States, and pro-American Middle Eastern countries were providing aid to the insurgents in 1979. The "unceasing armed intervention and far-reaching implications of the conspiracy of the external forces of reaction," Brezhnev commented on January 12, 1980, "created a real danger of Afghanistan losing its independence and being turned into an imperialist military bridgehead on our country's southern borders." Brezhnev also insisted that Russia had no "expansionist plans in respect to . . . other countries in that area." In short, Brezhnev appeared to believe that Afghanistan had been within the Soviet sphere of influence since 1978 and that intervention was necessary to preserve the Marxist revolution against domestic and foreign enemies.

Carter and Brzezinski were not willing to listen to, much less believe, any such self-serving explanations. To them, as to most Americans, it was a brutal invasion of an independent country, and the Soviet Union needed to be punished for it. Moreover, the timing was extremely poor. American pride had suffered a severe blow when, less than two months earlier, Iranian revolutionaries had seized the U.S. embassy in Teheran and taken more than fifty Americans hostage. Carter was under tremendous pressure to get the hostages back quickly or, if negotiations failed, to take military action against Iran. Moreover, the Marxist-dominated Sandinistas had come to power in July in Nicaragua and were developing close ties with Cuba; a controversy had developed in August and September about whether Russia had combat troops in Cuba and, if so, what the U.S. response should be; and the Organization of Petroleum Exporting Countries (OPEC) price hikes were again causing inflation at home and suggesting American impotence abroad. And now Russia was using its troops outside the Warsaw Pact area for the first time since World War II in order to shape Afghanistan's internal affairs. While one could argue about Angola or Ethiopia, the invasion of Afghanistan provided concrete evidence to support conservatives' warnings about "Soviet expansionism." Thus, even if Carter personally had favored a milder response, politically the 1979 chain of events and the effectiveness of the conservative critique of his earlier policies gave him virtually no choice but to take a strong stand against Russia.

The administration's hard-line response was both rhetorical and substantive. Carter and Brzezinski denounced the Soviet Union repeatedly over the next several weeks, saying that they were lying about their motives for invading Afghanistan. Carter also insisted that the Russian action "could pose the most serious threat to peace since the Second World War." Vance supported Carter's view that the Soviet invasion was "unacceptable" and that a strong U.S. response was required. But while Vance thought that Moscow's "immediate aim was to protect Soviet political interests in Afghanistan which they saw endangered," Brzezinski, now clearly Carter's chief adviser, believed that the Soviet action was "not a local but a strategic challenge." Carter agreed with Brzezinski, and in his State of the Union message to Congress on January 23 included a statement that quickly became known as the Carter Doctrine: "An attempt by any outside force to gain control of the Persian Gulf region will be regarded as an assault on the vital interests of the United States of America, and such an assault will be repelled by any means necessary, including military force."

The administration quickly decided on a series of measures designed to punish the Soviets for "their attempt to crush Afghanistan." On January 3, 1980, Carter asked the Senate to delay consideration of the SALT II treaty. The next day he announced several additional punitive measures. These included such economic measures as embargoes on the selling of grain and high-technology goods to the Soviets and such other actions as U.S. withdrawal from the 1980 summer Olympics in Moscow and the curtailment of cultural and scientific exchanges. The grain embargo was far from complete: eight million tons were sold in accordance with a 1975 agreement, and the seventeen million tons that were held back from the Soviets were largely obtained from Argentina and other nations, despite Carter's appeals to them not to increase their sales. In all, the State Department and the National Security Council came up with about forty steps the United States could take to punish Russia, and most of these were implemented. But several, including the Olympic boycott and the grain embargo, were controversial. The Republican presidential nominee, Ronald Reagan, told farmers that the embargo was hurting them, not the Russians, and that he would lift it if he became president.

Like previous Cold War crises, Afghanistan encouraged military approaches to containment and higher defense budgets. Carter asked Congress to approve increased defense spending (a growth of 5 percent above inflation) and registration of all 18-year-old males to make possible a rapid military buildup or a return to the draft. Combat readiness for existing forces was improved, and a Rapid Deployment Force that could intervene in the Persian Gulf or elsewhere began to be developed. The administration offered increased aid to Pakistan and other nations in the region and began close military collaboration with China. On July 25, 1980, Carter signed Presidential Directive 59, which put increased emphasis on targeting Soviet nuclear forces—a step widely seen as destabilizing mutual deterrence. Quickly leaked to the press, PD-59 epitomized Carter's hard-line stance during his last year in office. The president who had criticized Americans' "inordinate fear of communism" in 1977 had been virtually transformed into a Cold Warrior.

In many respects, the election of 1980 was a replay of 1976. As Ford had done with Reagan in 1976, Carter fought off a challenger from within his own party, Senator Edward M. Kennedy, to win the nomination. As with Ford, détente was no longer part of Carter's vocabulary. Like Carter four years earlier, Reagan won his party's nomination by defeating candidates—notably George Bush—who had considerable experience in Washington. During the fall campaign, the basic question was the same as in 1976: could an unpopular incumbent president, forced to defend his policies, defeat an outsider who was personally appealing but who lacked experience in national or world affairs? Like Carter in 1976, Reagan offered a positive vision of America as a nation of virtuous, old-fashioned patriots. He also promised to cut taxes, end inflation, strengthen the military, and stand up to the Russians and Iranians (who still held the hostages) better than Carter had been able to do. The situation was complicated by the presence of a significant third-party candidate, the liberal Republican, John Anderson, but the answer the voters gave was the same as in 1976: by a margin of 51 percent for Reagan to 41 percent for Carter, they elected a new president.

In regard to Soviet-American relations, there was one key difference between 1976 and 1980: whereas candidate Carter had largely supported détente, Reagan said that America should stop trying to make agreements with the untrustworthy Russians and "stand tall" against international communism. Whether his approach would work any better than Carter's, and what it would cost both financially and in relations with Russia and with America's allies, were key questions during Reagan's first few years in office.

Reagan and the Russians, 1981–1987

Leaders with new approaches to both domestic and world affairs came to power in the United States and the U.S.S.R. in the 1980s—Ronald Reagan in January 1981 and Mikhael Gorbachev in March 1985. Reagan's two main priorities were to cut taxes and to increase defense spending sharply while seeking congressional approval for major cuts in domestic programs. The 69-year-old president also believed that détente had failed and that the United States should return to a confrontational approach to the Soviet Union in which most world problems were seen in East-West terms.

Gorbachev, who was 54 when he assumed power, represented a new generation of Soviet leaders. Domestically, Gorbachev sought major changes to improve the sluggish Soviet economy, which required *glasnost* (openness to public debate) and *perestroika* (restructuring) to implement. In foreign affairs, the new leader favored improved relations with the West and offered bold proposals to reverse the arms race. While previous Soviet leaders had said they supported similar goals in foreign policy, Gorbachev had the public relations skills to gain widespread credibility in the West.

Both leaders insisted that their main goal was to make the world safer: Reagan primarily by creating a "margin of safety" in U.S. military power and by taking a tough stand against Russia and its allies (real and purported) in the Third World, and Gorbachev by proposals for partial disarmament. Whether the main goals of either leader will be achieved remains to be seen. For one thing, Reagan's "margin of safety," from the Soviet viewpoint, obviously meant a margin of superiority— something Moscow would not accept, intent as it was on full equality. Second, Reagan believed that military power and respect for America abroad were inseparable from economic strength. Yet, Reagan's tax and defense policies, while increasing the U.S. gross national product, resulted in a doubling (an increase of more than $1 trillion) in the federal government's indebtedness and contributed to America's shift from being a creditor nation in 1981 to becoming the world's largest debtor nation by 1986. Nor is it clear that his defense buildup increased either usable military power or America's standing in world affairs. And while there was considerable support for Gorbachev's policies both at home and abroad, it remains uncertain whether his domestic reforms will flourish in Russia's highly bureaucratic system or whether his proposals for a wide-ranging détente with the West will get very far.

Although the two leaders' place in history remains in doubt, both have contributed, in their different ways, to the intellectual ferment on defense issues that has characterized the 1980s. For the first time since the 1950s, serious questions have been raised about reliance on large numbers of nuclear weapons for defense. And people who have searched for safer ground beyond the current balance of terror—including the two leaders themselves—have not been dismissed as dreamers.

During his first term (January 1981–January 1985), Reagan, the former star of B-grade movies, was the leading actor on the world stage. At home, the president's personal charisma and leadership skills helped him to get both his big tax cuts and huge defense expenditures (an estimated $1.6 trillion over five years) through Congress. This money went for new and existing strategic programs and for expensive conventional programs such as expanding the navy from roughly 450 to 600 ships. Reagan also received large increases for the CIA and other intelligence agencies, partly to aid anti-Russian forces in Afghanistan and other Third World countries. Only for Central America—where Reagan wanted large sums to try to defeat the leftist insurgency in El Salvador and to help opposition forces topple the Marxist government in Nicaragua—did Congress appropriate significantly less money than the administration requested and limit Reagan's freedom of action in foreign affairs.

Abroad, the Reagan administration's ambitious efforts to implement its idealized image of the early days of the Cold War, when nations were thought to have followed America's lead as part of the "Free World" or to have suffered as enemies, were less successful. Most nations never had bowed meekly to American desires even at the height of the Cold War, and they certainly were not going to in the more pluralistic, equal atmosphere of the early 1980s. Administration officials such as Secretary of State Alexander Haig, who served in 1981–1982, insisted that Carter had failed to shape events abroad because he had lacked a coherent strategy and the will to implement it. The Reaganites thought they had a Cold War strategy, one reminiscent of NSC-68 (1950), and they took pride in their toughness. Like good actors, they got the attention of their audience and even frightened them at times with their loose rhetoric about how nuclear wars could be fought and won. The only problem was that foreigners refused to change their behavior to conform to administration plans. Thus, the limits of American power—a point that Nixon and Kissinger had grasped a decade before—were confirmed. These limits may be illustrated by looking briefly at U.S. relations in the early 1980s with Russia, Western Europe, and Central America.

Except for harsh rhetoric and a refusal to negotiate on arms control for more than a year, Reagan's administration did not have a consistent policy toward Russia. Reagan quickly lifted Carter's grain embargo but tried to tighten East-West trade further in other areas. Broadly speaking, the administration was divided between those who favored careful negotiations with Russia and those who strongly opposed any serious efforts to deal with "the enemy." The first group was centered in the State Department and included Haig; his successor, George Shultz; and the director of the State Department's Bureau of Politico-Military Affairs, Richard Burt. The second, often more powerful, faction included Secretary of Defense Caspar Weinberger, who wanted nothing—especially arms control—to jeopardize his military buildup; Richard Perle, the former assistant to Senator Jackson who served as assistant secretary of defense for international security affairs; CIA director William Casey; and the assistant secretary of state (later national security adviser), William Clark.

The "two Richards"—Burt and Perle—tangled repeatedly on arms control issues, with Burt willing and Perle unwilling to try to come up with proposals that the Soviets might accept. Reagan seemed to prefer making speeches about the "evil empire" to imposing specific policies on his quarreling subordinates, with the result that U.S. approach to the Soviet Union often featured more rhetoric than substance. Under pressure from West European leaders and from strong antinuclear movements in Europe and at home, the administration did begin negotiating with the Soviets in 1982. But Weinberger and Perle won the internal debate in the sense that the U.S. proposals on nuclear weapons were so one-sided that Russia was almost certain to reject them.

At first, Soviet leaders, thinking that Reagan's bark might be bigger than his bite, sought to strike a deal with the new president. They had generally experienced steadier relations with Republican than with Democratic administrations, and they thought that their relations with Reagan might follow this pattern. But the military buildup, the lack of interest in arms control, and talk by high officials about "going to the source" of aid to rebels in El Salvador and about the illegitimacy of Soviet rule in Eastern Europe and even in Russia frightened Soviet leaders into thinking that Reagan might attack their nation. Publicly, the succession of aging Soviet leaders in the early 1980s—Brezhnev, Yuri Andropov, and Konstantin Chernenko—said that they supported improved Soviet-American relations and urged Reagan to return to détente. Privately, it was learned several years later, the Soviets were so frightened by Washington's hard-line policies and rhetoric that the KGB

(Russia's main intelligence agency) was put on alert from 1981 to 1983.

Faced with U.S. hostility, the Soviets showed their determination to remain a superpower and protect their interests. In the absence of arms control, they said that they would maintain military strength equal to the United States. Despite veiled U.S. threats about Poland, where the Solidarity labor movement was challenging the government, the Soviets helped to insure that communist rule was maintained. Nor did they withdraw from Afghanistan or end their alliance with Cuba, as the Reagan administration would have liked.

One of the low points in postwar Soviet-American relations occurred when a Russian military plane shot down a South Korean civilian airliner flying over Soviet territory on September 1, 1983. The plane was traveling from Anchorage, Alaska, to Seoul, South Korea. All 269 passengers and crew aboard, including 61 Americans, were killed. In a televised address to the nation on September 2, Reagan denounced the "Korean airline massacre" as a "crime against humanity" for which "there was absolutely no justification, either legal or moral . . ." Other officials made similarly harsh statements, saying that the incident was typical of Soviet "barbarism." The Soviets responded that they believed the "intruder" had been a spy plane and that they had shot it down only after it failed to respond to Soviet inquiries concerning its identification. They pointed out that U.S. reconnaissance planes resembling the downed Boeing 747 frequently flew in or near their airspace and that a Korean airliner previously had been forced to land while flying over Soviet territory.

In the ensuing weeks U.S. officials, realizing that they could not substantiate their claims that Russia had deliberately shot down a civilian airliner, softened their rhetoric. But Soviet leaders remained incensed that U.S. leaders had used the incident to make virulent charges against them, and their anti-American rhetoric increased. On September 28 Andropov, then the top Soviet leader, issued one of the most strongly anti-American statements since the Stalin era. It accused the United

States of pursuing a "militarist course" designed to achieve "dominant positions in the world without reckoning with the interests of other states and peoples." Soviet leaders apparently decided that the U.S. response to the airliner incident, combined with the continuing lack of progress on arms control, offered conclusive proof that there was no point in continuing to seek to improve relations. That December they withdrew from the arms control negotiations in Geneva, thus leaving Soviet-American relations at low ebb until after the elections of 1984.

West European leaders also stood up to the Reagan administration when they disagreed with its policies. They reminded the president of their support for arms control as well as adequate defense expenditures, and they insisted that he follow through with NATO's pledge to try to remove the Soviet SS-20 missiles aimed at Western Europe through negotiations before installing new U.S. Pershing and cruise missiles in their countries. Reagan's response—agreeing to negotiate with the Russians and offering in November 1981 not to place any intermediate-range U.S. missiles in Western Europe if the Soviets dismantled theirs—helped to stem the growing influence of Europe's antinuclear movement.

While the United States and its NATO allies thus were able to patch over differences on arms control, conflicts relating to trade with Russia proved irreconcilable. To most West Europeans, economic détente should not be ended just because Russia did something they did not like. Thus, when the Carter administration decided in the wake of Afghanistan to curtail sales of computers and other high-technology goods to Russia, Western Europe had continued its own trade with Russia and, indeed, had picked up much of America's previous business. The Reagan administration did not approve of this trade and tried to stop some of it. The administration also did not like the fact that West Europeans planned to lend Russia money and sell it equipment to help build a pipeline to supply natural gas from Siberia to their countries.

In the spring and summer of 1982, the administration

moved toward a confrontation with the West Europeans on the latter issue. When Reagan ordered foreign subsidiaries of U.S. companies not to sell equipment for the pipeline and prohibited foreign companies from using American equipment or technology in the project, the Europeans were furious. They saw their own sovereignty being threatened by these efforts to tell their companies what they could and could not do, and they pointed out that they had received the licenses to use the U.S. technology before Reagan was elected and thus were operating within their legal rights. As British Prime Minister Margaret Thatcher, normally a close ally, commented: "The question is whether one very powerful nation can prevent existing contracts from being fulfilled. I think it is wrong to do that." Eventually the United States had to back down on this issue, and Secretary of State Shultz had to work to ease tempers and to reach some vague face-saving agreements for the United States.

Beginning in early 1981, the administration also chose confrontation as the keynote of its policy in Central America and the Caribbean. Haig and other officials did not believe that Carter had been sufficiently forceful in dealing with this region, which Reagan described as a "Red lake." The new administration ridiculed Carter's emphasis on human rights in Latin America as naive and blamed him for the rise to power of the Sandinistas in Nicaragua in 1979. Seeing a concrete opportunity to break with "the failed policies of the past" and to establish itself as a vigorous opponent of communism, the Reagan administration moved quickly to shape events in Central America.

El Salvador is a small, poor country long ruled by and largely for the economic benefit of a wealthy elite. A revolutionary movement calling for greater economic equality had gained strength in the 1970s and was waging a guerrilla war against the government. Carter had sought to encourage land reform and an end to right-wing death squads while also opposing the guerrillas. Reagan, however, ignored the unsavory record of the right, which had included the murders of the

Catholic archbishop, Oscar Romero, and of four American nuns working to help the poor. Instead, the administration focused on defeating the rebels. To build a case for greater U.S. involvement, the State Department hastily issued a "White Paper" in February 1981. It blamed "Cuba, the Soviet Union, and other Communist states" for El Salvador's political instability and claimed that Nicaragua was a major supplier of arms to the leftist forces. It seemed likely that Nicaragua did provide some military aid to the rebels, as U.S. officials repeatedly charged, but the administration had difficulty in offering convincing evidence to prove it. Under Reagan, U.S. aid to El Salvador was increased, most of the economic and political inequities remained, and the guerrillas never came close to toppling the government.

Once the situation in El Salvador had more or less stabilized, Reagan's main goal in the region—though never officially acknowledged—became the overthrow of the Nicaraguan government. Reagan did not like the Sandinistas' Marxist orientation, and he especially did not like their close ties with Cuba and Russia. To overthrow the Sandinistas, the administration tried almost everything it could think of except direct U.S. military intervention.

The administration was not lacking in persistence. It cut off aid to and trade with Nicaragua; it made it difficult for Nicaragua to obtain loans from international agencies; and it sent the CIA to mine Nicaraguan harbors and otherwise to disrupt the economy. Most important, it supplied weapons and money to an army of Nicaraguans in exile (the contras), sent U.S. forces to train them in Honduras, and persuaded wealthy conservatives and U.S. allies to supply additional arms and money to them. When Congress finally cut off U.S. aid to the contras in 1985, the president's staff continued raising money from domestic and foreign sources and came up with a new scheme: giving the contras some of the profits from the secret sale of U.S. arms to Iran.

Why did all these efforts fail to overthrow the Nicaraguan government? The main reason was that most Nicaraguans supported the government, which was given credit for toppling the Somoza family dictatorship and which was providing education, health care, and more equitable access to land. Unlike Somoza, the Sandinistas were willing to arm the common people, who consistently defeated contra troops and drove them back to their camps in Honduras and Costa Rica. Unlike Cuba and Russia, Nicaragua permitted private businesses to play a major role in the economy and opposition parties to compete in elections. While there were human rights abuses and restrictions on the press, the Sandinistas were far from being the worst offenders in Latin America. Other reasons for the failure of Reagan's policy included the lack of significant support for the contras inside the country, even among those who opposed the Sandinistas; sympathy for Nicaragua's right to self-determination in Latin America (especially in Mexico) and in Western Europe; and, of course, economic and military aid from Cuba and Russia. Because many of the contra leaders were former members of Somoza's hated police force (the National Guard) and because they have quarreled bitterly among themselves while failing to articulate a positive vision for Nicaragua's future, it was probably not in the cards that they should come to power.

Reagan did succeed in removing the Marxist government of Grenada in late 1983. A tiny island nation in the Caribbean, Grenada received its independence from Great Britain in 1974. Its corrupt and repressive leader, Eric Gairy, was overthrown in a leftist coup in 1979 led by Maurice Bishop. The Carter administration was angered when Grenada (along with Nicaragua and Cuba) did not vote in the United Nations to condemn the Soviet invasion of Afghanistan, and both Carter and Reagan were upset by Bishop's close ties to Cuba. The leaders of some of the neighboring islands also disliked Bishop's disdain for democratic procedures and his ties to Cuba.

Why did the United States invade Grenada on October 25, 1983, and, having won a quick military victory against local and Cuban troops, install a pro-American government a few days later? A coup against Bishop by one of his assistants in mid-October had thrown the country into turmoil, and there was some concern about the safety of Americans enrolled in a medical school on the island. But the main reason seems to be that Reagan wanted to "win one for the Gipper": he sought to defeat and then expel the government's Cuban advisers and put Grenada back on America's side. He also wanted a decisive victory to make up for the recent terrorist attack on the Marine barracks in Lebanon, which had killed 230 Americans. Reagan apparently reasoned, correctly as it turned out, that he would have much greater support in U.S. public opinion and in the Caribbean for a brief involvement in troubled Grenada than for a U.S.-led invasion of Nicaragua. The only sour note for the triumphant president occurred when journalists and other commentators noted parallels between the U.S. invasion of Grenada and Soviet actions in Afghanistan.

Following Grenada, Reagan's approval rating shot up and it continued high until 1986. But 1984–like 1964 for Johnson and 1972 for Nixon—was Reagan's year of triumph. At home, the recession that had hurt his popularity earlier was over, and the economy was growing rapidly without inflation. Abroad, U.S. policy had experienced both successes and failures, as usual, but Reagan (unlike Carter) seemed to know how to receive full credit for the successes and to keep the failures from hurting him politically. Supporters of an effort to freeze nuclear weapons systems as a first step toward disarmament had gained considerable public support in 1982 and 1983, but they could not get leading Democratic presidential contenders to campaign actively on this issue because Reagan's "peace through strength" approach seemed more popular with the general public. Moreover, Reagan shrewdly softened his rhetoric toward the Soviets and reminded voters of his commitment to peace. Although no Democrat stood much of a chance in 1984, the party virtually insured a landslide Reagan victory by nominating Carter's vice president, Walter Mondale, as its candidate. Most voters had vivid memoirs of inflation, Iran, and their general disappointment with Carter, and they overwhelmingly elected Reagan for a second term in November 1984.

Like most other presidents reelected by huge margins, Reagan ran into serious difficulties in his second term. He remained highly popular with the general public until revelations about sales of arms to Iran and the diversion of funds to the contras began to appear in late 1986. But even earlier Americans with the greatest interest in public affairs—including journalists and politicians of both parties—tended to become more openly skeptical about Reagan and his policies than they had been during his first term. Persistent questions were aired: Was Reagan knowledgeable about foreign policy issues? Was he in control of his administration? Was the defense buildup costing too much? Was the Pentagon using the huge appropriations wisely? Were Reagan's policies contributing to unprecedented budget and trade deficits? Was the president's protection of his anti-ballistic missile "Star Wars" defense plan worth the failure to reach agreements on arms control? And, finally, was the Iran-contra scandal another Watergate requiring the president's resignation or impeachment?

In East-West relations—especially arms control—Reagan lost the initiative to the dynamic new Soviet leader, Gorbachev. Earlier, Reagan had outflanked Americans and Europeans clamoring for arms control by agreeing to negotiate and, equally important, by coming up with a new source of contention: the Strategic Defense Initiative (SDI), popularly known as "Star Wars." In his television address announcing his proposal on March 23, 1983, the president presented his "vision" of a world without nuclear weapons and asked: "What if free people could live secure in the knowledge that their security did not rest upon the threat of instant U.S. retaliation to deter a Soviet attack; that we could intercept and destroy strategic ballistic missiles before they reached our own soil and that of our allies?"

It was a lofty vision, a hope that the mutual balance of terror could be overcome by a unilateral U.S. program that could render Russia's missiles useless in war. The problem was that only Reagan, some conservatives, and those who would be working on the program in the defense establishment seemed to think that it could work. Others agreed that it might be possible to protect some missile sites, as had been known since the 1960s, but few believed that it could protect populations against a major Soviet attack. Former Defense Secretary Harold Brown, for example, wrote that it was technically impossible to protect populations before at least the year 2010. Others maintained that Soviet offensive countermeasures probably could negate "Star Wars" indefinitely, and at much lower cost. Opponents also argued that any major testing or deployment would violate the ABM treaty (1972), the most successful and durable arms agreement negotiated to date. But

Reagan remained firm in his support, and Congress appropriated money for research.

It was Reagan's unswerving support for "Star Wars" and other military programs that enabled Gorbachev to seize the initiative soon after his accession to power in the spring of 1985. Knowing that most West Europeans saw Reagan's program as a pointless escalation of the arms race, Gorbachev not only denounced "Star Wars" but also took concrete steps to demonstrate Russia's interest in more peaceful relations. He announced a moratorium on underground nuclear testing and reduced the number of SS-20 missiles aimed at Western Europe. In renewed Soviet-American negotiations on arms control, Russia offered to make deep cuts in its missiles if the U.S. would stop its research on "Star Wars." Gorbachev also arranged a summit meeting with Reagan, held in Geneva November 19–21, 1985. As expected, SDI was a major source of contention, and little progress was made on arms control. Increasingly, Reagan was held responsible. As columnist Tom Wicker wrote in the *New York Times* on November 25, "President Reagan's Strategic Defense Initiative is the principal barrier to the 50 percent reductions in each superpower's nuclear arsenal that the two leaders agreed in principle to pursue."

As Gorbachev's peace offensive continued into 1986, Reagan ran into growing difficulties with Congress and with European allies. In mid-January, the Soviet leader appealed to all nations having nuclear weapons to eliminate them in stages by the year 2000. More concretely, he extended the Soviet moratorium on nuclear tests for another three months and asked the United States to join it. But Reagan appeared to be moving in the opposite direction: on May 27 he announced that his administration would no longer promise to observe the SALT II limits on offensive weapons.

This announcement stirred a storm of protest in Congress and among former high officials. Buoyed by public opinion polls that showed support for observing SALT II running two-to-one, the House of Representatives voted on June 19 to urge Reagan to adhere to SALT II limits as long as the Russians continued to do so. Respected former officials such as Robert McNamara and foreign leaders such as Margaret Thatcher also urged Reagan to abide by the SALT limits. Although Congress made major cuts in the president's "Star Wars" budget requests, the administration proceeded to develop a new interpretation of the ABM treaty that, in its view, permitted it to test SDI.

In early 1986, both America and Russia suffered disturbing, highly publicized failures of technology that, while not involved in their bilateral relations, caused a decline in prestige abroad. On January 28, the U.S. space shuttle *Challenger* exploded and crashed shortly after takeoff, killing its seven crew members and raising doubts about the future of the manned space program. And, on April 26, an explosion and fire at the Soviet nuclear power plant at Chernobyl (near Kiev) resulted in the deaths of at least thirty persons and spread poisonous radiation across much of Europe. To many observers, the *Challenger* tragedy called into question Reagan's faith in technology, as exemplified in "Star Wars." And Russia's early efforts to cover up the Chernobyl disaster—including its failure to issue warnings about the danger of radiation—angered Western Europeans and lessened their respect for Gorbachev.

Meanwhile, Soviet-American relations cooled after the 1985 Geneva summit as the two sides remained far apart on arms control. As before, the U.S. wanted deep cuts in Soviet land-based missiles, and Russia sought an end to SDI as part of any deal. Faced with congressional hostility to his statement that the United States would abandon its pledge of compliance with SALT II, Reagan softened his rhetoric on that issue, but he remained firm on SDI. In a speech on June 19, he described SDI as a "shield that could protect us from nuclear missiles just as a roof protects a family from rain." Despite continuing differences, plans for a second summit appeared to be moving forward until August 23, when the FBI set a trap for a Soviet official at the United Nations, Gennady Zakharov, and arrested him on accusations of spying. The Soviets then set a trap for an American journalist in Moscow, Nicholas Daniloff, and arrested him on similar charges. Believing—probably correctly—that Daniloff had been framed, U.S. officials and journalists were incensed, and anti-Soviet stories proliferated in the media until Zakharov and Daniloff were both freed in late September. At that point the two sides announced that a summit would be held in Reykjavik, Iceland, on October 11–12.

The meeting at Reykjavik was perhaps the most remarkable of the many Soviet-American summits since 1943. Reagan seemed to think that the meetings were exploratory, and he was not fully prepared for serious bargaining. But Gorbachev had come to deal, and he challenged Reagan to try to negotiate a comprehensive arms control agreement that weekend. Gorbachev offered significant concessions. He agreed in principle to the 1981 U.S. proposal to eliminate medium-range missiles from Europe and suggested a roughly 50 percent cut in strategic weapons on both sides over the next five years. In the climactic session on Sunday, Reagan proposed eliminating all ballistic missiles within ten years, and Gorbachev responded that the two sides should abolish not just their missiles but all their nuclear weapons. "That suits me fine," Reagan replied. But then Gorbachev made it clear that his agreement to any deal was premised on confining work on SDI to the "laboratory." Reagan said that this restriction would "kill" SDI and, when Gorbachev refused to budge from his position, Reagan gathered up his papers and left. Forced to choose between "Star Wars" and a deal that might end the Soviet nuclear threat through disarmament, Reagan's basic unilateralism and distrust of Russia won out.

The political fallout from Reykjavik lasted for several weeks. Liberals praised the two leaders for their efforts to reverse or even end the nuclear arms race and urged them to make the necessary compromises to conclude a treaty. Conservatives were grateful that Reagan had stood firm on SDI but expressed concern that he had offered to trade away America's nuclear deterrent. Both the Pentagon and NATO allies were upset because they had not been consulted about proposals that would, if implemented, bring drastic changes in the West's defense posture.

During the remainder of 1986 and the first half of 1987, Reagan followed the two-track approach that he had been pursuing since 1982: build up America's strategic arsenal and negotiate on arms control. On the first track, the Pentagon openly violated the SALT limits on November 28, 1986, when it put cruise missiles on the 131st B-52 bomber (130 had been permitted under the treaty). Concerned that congressional support for SDI might decline if components of the system were not tested before Reagan left office, the Pentagon pushed in early 1987 for a demonstration of one such component—a move that most experts insisted would violate the ABM treaty. On the arms control track, Russia retained the initiative: on February 28, 1987, Gorbachev offered to separate the European intermediate-range missile issue from strategic and space weapons issues and said that he supported the long-standing U.S. proposal to remove all Soviet and U.S. intermediate-range missiles from Europe. Reagan responded positively to Gorbachev's speech, and talks continued over the next several months.

Aided by public and congressional pressure and by an overall trend toward greater cooperation between the superpowers, these negotiations were successful. On September 18, 1987, Secretary of State George Shultz and Soviet Foreign Minister Eduard Shevardnadze announced an "agreement in principle to conclude a treaty" that would require the elimination of approximately 1,000 U.S. and Soviet land-based missiles with ranges of between 310 and 3,200 miles. Reagan and Gorbachev were expected to meet to sign the treaty later in the fall.

As a percentage of the total nuclear weapons possessed by both nations, the reduction was modest: roughly 2,000 warheads, or 5 percent of the combined arsenals. Yet the agreement, if fully implemented, will be highly significant for two reasons. For the first time, the superpowers will have agreed to remove substantial numbers of missiles and nuclear warheads, thus setting a precedent for reducing the arsenals further in the future. And second, Reagan will have become the sixth consecutive president, starting with Kennedy, to reach an arms control agreement with the Soviet Union. Efforts to increase security through negotiations would appear to be a normal feature of Soviet-American relations.

Conclusion

Ordinary Americans following developments in Soviet-American relations from 1973 to 1987 never knew quite what to expect. One week their president might be hailing a breakthrough in arms control or East-West trade and the next week he might be denouncing Soviet involvement in some previously obscure Third World country or saying that American troops had landed somewhere because of the threat posed by a nation that was receiving military aid from Russia. An article in the newspaper would say that the United States was ahead in the arms race, but on the next page there would be another news story warning that America was falling dangerously behind.

The reality beneath the confusing headlines was that there were elements of both competition and cooperation in Soviet-American relations, as there had been throughout the Cold War. In the early 1970s, when détente was at its peak, an effort was made to strike a new, enduring balance between competition and cooperation in order to try to prevent the dangerously competitive behavior that had threatened to lead to war on several occasions between 1946 and 1962. In this narrow sense, détente appears to have succeeded: the two nations were able to keep further away from war during the crises of the fifteen years after 1972 than they had during the crises of the fifteen years before 1963.

Still, détente largely failed in the broader sense of establishing a relationship in which (a) the arms race and expenditures on defense would be brought under meaningful control;

(b) competition in the Third World would decrease significantly; and (c) trade would increase steadily and serve to stabilize Soviet-American relations. The reason détente failed is at once complex and simple: complex in that many factors were involved, but simple in that both nations continued to view the relationship in largely competitive terms. This was certainly true of the military establishments (and their vocal supporters) on both sides, which were not content with the destructive power and sophistication of the arsenals in 1972 but instead undermined the arms control process by using it as a pretext to push ahead with even more dangerous systems. Intense competition also continued in the Third World, where each side rightly accused the other of a lack of restraint and a disregard for the principle of self-determination. Although Soviet-American trade never stopped entirely, it became a political football and thus largely weighed on the competitive side of the scales.

If leaders on both sides ever want to try to build a relationship that might realize more of the early promise of détente, they can learn much about what *not* to do by careful study of the years 1973 to 1987.

Can the Cold War Be Ended?

In a very real sense, the world no longer has a choice between force and law. If civilization is to survive, it must choose the rule of law.

> Dwight D. Eisenhower,
> proclamation of first Law Day,
> May 1, 1958

... the modern world has become much too small and fragile for wars and policy of force. It cannot be saved and preserved

if the thinking and actions built up over the centuries on the
acceptability and permissibility of wars and armed conflicts
are not shed once and for all. . . . [If the arms race continues]
The situation in the world may assume such a character that
it will no longer depend upon the intelligence or will of
political leaders. It may become captive to technology, to
technocratic military logic.

Mikhail Gorbachev,
speech to Soviet Communist Party Congress,
February 25, 1986

May there always be sunshine
May there always be blue skies
May there always be Mama
May there always be me.

Russian child's prayer

In 1986 two eminent Harvard professors, political scientist
Richard E. Neustadt and historian Ernest R. May, published
a book entitled *Thinking in Time: The Uses of History for
Decision Makers.* The authors argued that more wise and effective policies tend to be pursued when leaders cultivate the
practice of "seeing time as a stream"—that is, viewing the present and future as growing out of the past and visualizing how
a policy proposal, if adopted, might fit into the stream of history years or even decades later. One example they offer is
George Marshall, who, as secretary of state in the late 1940s,
drew upon his "habit of thought about time as a stream" in
supporting economic assistance to Europe and opposing military intervention in the Chinese civil war.

Like policymakers, students of history need to see time
as a stream, to gain a sense of how the present has grown out
of the past and how it is pointing toward a future that, like
previous futures, will contain both predictable and surprising
features. In applying the time-stream metaphor to the Cold
War, this epilogue focuses on two questions. Looking first from

the past to the present, what has changed since the 1940s to make the Soviet-American rivalry quite different now than it was forty years ago? And then peering more tentatively toward the future, how might the relationship be made more stable with greater emphasis on cooperation and less on competition and conflict? If the brief answers offered here provoke thought and discussion while helping to tie together some of the information in the previous chapters, they will have served their purpose.

As John Lewis Gaddis has noted, the international order that America and Russia took the lead in establishing after 1945 has been much more durable than other modern efforts to establish peace, notably the attempt at Versailles in 1919. Despite numerous crises, the two nations have carefully avoided war with each other, and they remain the two most powerful nations on earth and the leaders of the only significant military alliances, NATO and the Warsaw Pact. Yet so much has changed since the late 1940s—both internationally and within each superpower—that the currents of history clearly are moving away from the bipolar Cold War pattern. At least six key changes have occurred.

First, the remarkable development and proliferation of military technology, often initiated by the United States, has had the effect of lessening America's relative military power dramatically. In the late 1940s, only the United States had nuclear weapons; as late as the early 1960s, the United States still possessed the vast majority of the world's nuclear weapons and delivery systems. By the late 1970s, Russia had pulled relatively even with the United States, and Britain, France, and China had significant nuclear arsenals. Moreover, conventional armaments had become more sophisticated, more destructive, and more widespread among both industrial and preindustrial nations. One result of the proliferation of both nuclear and conventional weapons is that it is now more dangerous for big nations to take military actions against smaller countries—as Russia (in Afghanistan) and the United States (in Lebanon) were reminded in the 1980s.

Second, for the first time in history, the idea of war between the two greatest powers (in this case, the United States and Russia) has become extremely irrational. In the past, wars between great powers frequently have been initiated because one side or the other thought that it could advance its national interest and increase its power through war. In the late 1940s, before Russia built the bomb, some U.S. military planners viewed the atomic bomb as "the winning weapon," and Truman thought about dropping nuclear weapons on Russia and China during the Korean War. The situation changed in the 1950s, however, when Russia acquired operational nuclear weapons: Eisenhower and all subsequent presidents have stressed the impossibility of winning a nuclear war in any meaningful sense; the same has been true of all Soviet leaders since Stalin.

The fact that all-out wars between nuclear powers almost certainly would result in mutual suicide for their societies has given rise to several paradoxes largely new in human history: the largest military establishments in history, those of America and Russia, can do virtually nothing to protect their nation's security against an attack by the other; these two nations, which have spent the most on nuclear weaponry, are the ones most likely to be totally devastated if deterrence fails; and countries which have chosen not to build nuclear weapons or have allies station them on their territory, thus from one viewpoint rendering them defenseless, in fact are the countries least likely to be attacked with nuclear weapons in the event of war. One more paradox: while the effects of the large-scale use of nuclear weapons clearly would be horrible, their presence may have helped to maintain peace among the nations possessing them since 1945 because of the caution induced by their unprecedented destructive power.

These paradoxes suggest that, for countries defended by nuclear weapons and for the many others which would be affected by fallout and other environmental damage, the weapons simultaneously pose a huge danger to everyone involved, thus making the world more interdependent than ever before, while lessening the immediate risks of war as long as sanity prevails among those controlling the weapons or a tragic accident leading to a nuclear exchange does not occur. Clearly, the premises of great-power relations are different from what they were before the nuclear age: what is now at stake is less national security in the traditional sense than the security of humanity as a whole (often referred to as common security). As long as there are large numbers of nuclear weapons, peace is the only realistic choice.

Third, since the late 1940s and early 1950s, when Russian and American leaders were barely talking to each other, the two nations have found many areas of common interest, thus easing Cold War tensions. In addition to their bilateral arms control agreements, they have cooperated on multilateral ones like the nonproliferation treaty of 1968. And while the United States refused for decades to have diplomatic or trade relations with China and Cuba, the United States and Russia have maintained a wide range of economic, scientific, and cultural relationships since the mid-1950s. It is significant—and perhaps suggestive for the future—that the United States and Russia did not have a military confrontation during the downturn in relations in the late 1970s and early 1980s, in contrast to their experience during the previous two dangerous phases.

A fourth trend since the late 1940s has been the growing influence and assertiveness of nations other than America and Russia, thus leading to a diffusion of power away from the two postwar giants. The economic recovery of Western Europe, Japan, and other nations has led to a decline in America's GNP as a percentage of world GNP from about 50 percent to about 20 percent; the countries of Western Europe, which the United States helped with the Marshall Plan, now have a greater combined GNP than the United States. The United States has shifted from being the world's great creditor nation to the world's leading debtor nation; Japanese and other wealthy foreigners bought hundreds of billions of dollars of bonds to help finance the Reagan administration's defense buildup and budget deficits in the 1980s. Overall, America's major allies are much more independent in their thinking and actions than they were in the 1940s, a trend that is almost certain to continue. And, given the fact that nuclear weapons cannot be used to achieve political ends, the diffusion of power is likely to persist.

Except militarily, Russia likewise no longer exerts the influence abroad that it did in the 1940s. Nationalism has proven to be stronger than communism in the sense that most communist parties no longer look to Moscow for guidance. That is the case not only for countries that have broken openly with Russia—notably Yugoslavia and China—but also for communist parties in Western Europe. Even in the Eastern European countries where Soviet troops remain, there is considerable variation in economic and political practice from country to country. Like America, Russia faces the embarrassing fact that its per capita GNP has fallen behind that of some of its allies. Given their falling economic status and the decline in deference to their ideas, perhaps the two nations should form a Superpower Protective Association to promote their interests!

Fifth, there have been major shifts in Russia since the death of Stalin away from one-man rule, from total direction of the economy from Moscow, and toward greater openness to outside ideas. Although there remains much to criticize from a Western viewpoint, there has been, as Kennan predicted in 1947, a "gradual mellowing of Soviet power." One must always be careful in using official rhetoric as historical evidence; yet the differences in both tone and substance of Stalin's addresses in 1946 and Gorbachev's in 1986 are truly remarkable, suggesting less defensiveness and narrow-minded nationalism and more willingness to admit mistakes and to initiate political and economic reforms.

Finally, there has been a decline in America's consistency and sense of common purpose in foreign affairs. The Cold War consensus could lead to mistakes, such as the involvement in

Vietnam and the effort to ostracize communist China; but at
its best it offered a vision of an interdependent world in which
the United States would take the lead in assuring both security
and economic progress. In so doing, the United States would
cooperate with others through institutions like the United Nations, the International Monetary Fund, the World Bank, and
NATO. Since the mid-1960s, U.S. foreign policy has tended
to be less consistent and consultative, more dependent on the
preferences of whoever has happened to be president than on
a broad base of informed opinion. Admittedly, the world has
become more complex and choosing the proper policies has
been more difficult at a time when conservative and liberal
views often have diverged sharply. Yet poor leadership also
has played a role, thus raising concerns about how Americans
select their leaders. One question has been asked repeatedly
in recent years, both at home and abroad: can the United States
afford the luxury of electing presidents with no experience in
either the federal government or foreign affairs, as happened
in 1976 and again in 1980?

Despite recent difficulties in Soviet-American relations,
the overall trend since the late 1940s and early 1950s has been
toward greater stability and cooperation. How might this trend
be encouraged in the future, such that some of the sharp ups
and downs of the past might be avoided and the huge defense
expenditures on both sides be cut back? How might the competition in the Third World—the source of much distrust recently—be lessened?

While recognizing that historians often make poor proph-
ets, I believe that current conditions favor a continuing improvement in Soviet-American relations. Just as East-West
issues made the front pages less frequently in 1986–1987 than
they did in the early 1960s (a period I have studied in detail),
my guess is that East-West issues will be even less prominent
in the year 2000.

On nuclear weapons and delivery systems, the reality of
common security suggests that negotiated agreements are in

the national interest of both countries, as U.S. and Soviet leaders (except Reagan during his first term) have realized since the late 1960s. The quest for superiority in offensive weapons is both expensive and pointless when both sides have such large numbers, and no defensive system could provide unilateral security against an adversary determined to maintain rough equality. Both reason and economics point toward ending the nuclear buildup, followed by a gradual build-down to a smaller deterrent force: reason, because building more weapons decreases security by threatening the deterrent capability of the other side and by increasing the probable devastation if deterrence ever failed; and economics, because Russian leaders want to put their resources into increasing consumer goods and generally modernizing their economy, whereas the U.S. government must stop borrowing money from abroad to pay its bills and American corporations need to focus on improving their competitiveness in consumer goods instead of having their best engineers work on military projects. In short, once U.S. leaders and the public grasp the reality of common security and the full economic costs of the Reagan buildup, serious negotiations to stabilize the relationship and to prevent the deployment of new systems may well be possible.

Many specific proposals for lessening the danger of nuclear war have gained wide support in recent years. One of the most promising is the idea of having a joint Soviet-American crisis control center in Geneva, or ones in Moscow and Washington, designed to lessen the risk of an accidental war. Because satellite reconnaissance is crucial to each side's intelligence-gathering capability, many arms control experts have proposed that testing of antisatellite weapons should be prohibited; and because submarines provide the securest deterrent force (they are not as vulnerable to attack as land-based missiles), efforts to improve antisubmarine warfare should be limited. If it can be agreed that nuclear weapons only make sense for deterrence of war and not for actual war-fighting, these and related proposals (such as ending all testing of nuclear weapons) might be implemented quickly.

America and Russia also could save money on defense by cutting back their forces in Europe. Both nations have hundreds of thousands of troops stationed there; yet for more than two decades Europe—especially Western Europe—has been one of the most politically stable and prosperous areas in the world. Because the U.S. presence has contributed to this stability, it probably would be wise to maintain some troops there, if the West Europeans continue to want them. But with Britain and France as nuclear powers and with West Germany having strong conventional forces and the wealth to do even more, it would appear that the U.S. could cut back its role safely. Russia might be more reluctant to risk its informal empire in Eastern Europe; but a partial withdrawal could improve relations with the West and signal to the East Europeans that Russia is less inclined to intervene in their internal affairs than it was earlier in the Cold War.

These two steps—stabilizing the nuclear balance and pulling back partially from Europe—could improve Soviet-American relations substantially. But progress also will be needed in limiting the competition in the Third World before the Cold War can be said to be over. Yet this may be the most difficult nut to crack, because both nations are heavily involved in volatile regions like the Middle East and because Americans resent Soviet competition in areas in which, until the 1960s, the United States and its allies were the main outside actors. It also is difficult to establish rules of the game to limit competition in the Third World, short of both nations' agreeing to stay out entirely. Often it is preferable to search for multilateral solutions, as with the U.N. peacekeeping operations in the Middle East before 1967 or the Contadora process in Central America in the 1980s, but these can break down or be ineffective.

If U.S. and Soviet involvement in the Third World declines in the near future, it may well result as much as anything from financial considerations. There are indications that Gorbachev is taking a hard look at the costs of supporting Cuba, Vietnam, and other allies in the Third World, as well as the expense of the war in Afghanistan. The United States, similarly, may be forced to think about whether it can afford to send billions of dollars each year to Israel, Egypt, and various "freedom fighters" around the world who have grown accustomed to receiving American aid. The United States could afford to do these things when it had trade surpluses and controlled a large percentage of the world's financial resources; whether it can continue to do so while running trade deficits and borrowing huge sums from abroad remains to be seen. And there is the further question, raised anew by the Iran-contra affair, of whether covert activities abroad are consistent with America's system of checks and balances, its belief in the rule of law, and the need for public understanding and support if a foreign policy is to succeed over time.

For improved Soviet-American relations to endure and become the normal expectation, leaders in Moscow will need to bridge the gap between their prodétente statements and actions that have undermined it—for example, the invasion of Afghanistan. They also will need to improve their human rights practices and permit more open debate and the airing of weaknesses in Soviet society—all of which have occurred under Gorbachev to an extent unimaginable as recently as the early 1980s. Leaders in Washington, for their part, must stop talking and acting as if they are the world's repository of wisdom and virtue, and acknowledge that the United States bears considerable responsibility for the nuclear arms race and for the recent violence in Central America. Finally, the American people will need to recognize that both competition and cooperation will continue in Soviet-American relations, as in U.S. dealings with other countries, and that particular disagreements need not signal a renewed Cold War. The public also must stop rewarding presidential candidates (e.g., Kennedy in 1960 and Reagan in 1980) who falsely claim that the incumbent administration has permitted the United States to fall behind the Soviets in the arms race.

Much of what happens in Soviet-American relations for the remainder of the century will depend on the younger generation of leaders who gradually are assuming power in both countries. Unlike the major leaders on both sides between 1945 and the early 1980s, most of these new leaders are neither veterans of World War II nor active participants in the bitter competition of the early Cold War years. Their experience of superpower relations thus is mixed: they recall the period of relative détente in the 1960s and early 1970s, and they also remember the downturn in Soviet-American relations in the late 1970s and early 1980s.

If these new leaders in both nations are able to "think in time" and recognize their common interests—increasing trade and cultural contacts, developing ways to limit Soviet-American conflict in the Third World, and, above all, lessening the danger of nuclear war—they may be able to break the cycle of continuing year after year to fear, denounce, and prepare to destroy each other. If and when that occurs, the Cold War will indeed be over.

BIBLIOGRAPHICAL ESSAY

A comprehensive and critical bibliographical essay on the Cold War—one involving discussion of the thousands of books, articles, and available primary sources which have contributed to understanding this huge subject—would require another book longer than this one. Accordingly, I have limited myself primarily to books which I have found especially useful in preparing this study. I also have chosen, given limitations on space, to include for student reference a relatively large number of books rather than commenting critically on each of a much smaller number.

For a general introduction to the literature on Soviet-American relations, including some discussion of primary sources, see the bibliographical essay in John Lewis Gaddis, *Russia, the Soviet Union, and the United States: An Interpretive History* (1978). A more detailed listing of books and articles relating to the Cold War years is contained in two book-length bibliographies: E. David Cronon and Theodore D. Rosenof, *The Second World War and the Atomic Age, 1940–1973* (1975), pp. 8–48, and William B. Fowler, *American Diplomatic History since 1890* (1975), pp. 108–54. The most complete, annotated bibliography is Richard Dean Burns, ed., *Guide to American Foreign Relations since 1700* (1983), pp. 699–1213.

General Works

Four general studies which I found particularly helpful in writing this book are Adam B. Ulam, *The Rivals: America and Russia since World War II* (1971); Joseph G. Whelan, *Soviet Diplomacy and Negotiating Behavior: Emerging New Context for U.S. Diplomacy* (1979); John Lewis Gaddis, *Strategies of Containment* (1982); and chapters 6–9 in the book by Gaddis listed above.

Several other general accounts and collections of essays also were quite useful: Stephen E. Ambrose, *Rise to Globalism: American Foreign Policy, 1938–1980* (1980); Richard J. Barnet, *The Giants: Russia and America* (1977); Seyom Brown, *The Faces of Power: Constancy and Change in United States Foreign Policy from Truman to Reagan* (1983); Lawrence Freedman, *The Evolution of Nuclear Strategy* (1981); Mark Garrison and Abbott Gleason, eds., *Shared Destiny; Fifty Years of Soviet-American Relations* (1985); Louis J. Halle, *The Cold War as History* (1967); Bennett Korvig, *The Myth of Liberation: East-Central Europe in U.S. Diplomacy and Politics since 1941* (1973); Walter LaFeber, *America, Russia, and the Cold War, 1945–1984* (1984); Werner Link, *The East-West Conflict* (1986); Michael Mandelbaum, *The Nuclear Question* (1979); Earnest R. May, *"Lessons" of the Past: The Use and Misuse of History in American Foreign Policy* (1973); Frank J. Merli and Theodore A. Wilson, eds., *Makers of American Diplomacy: From Theodore Roosevelt to Henry Kissinger* (1974); Ronald Steel, *Pax Americana* (1967); and John B. Stoessinger, *Crusaders and Pragmatists: Movers of Modern American Foreign Policy* (1979).

Two outstanding books focusing on Soviet foreign policy are Adam B. Ulam, *Expansion and Coexistence: The History of Soviet Foreign Policy, 1917–1973* (1974) and Erik P. Hoffman and Frederick J. Fleron, Jr., eds., *The Conduct of Soviet Foreign Policy* (1980). For the Soviet viewpoint, see B. Ponomaryov et al., eds., *History of Soviet Foreign Policy*, 2 vols.

(1969 and 1974); and Nikolai V. Sivachev and Nikolai N. Yakovlev, *Russia and the United States* (1979). Peter Calvocoressi, *World Politics since 1945* (1977), provides a British perspective on the Cold War era.

General accounts of relations between the United States and China, with varying degrees of coverage of the years since 1949, include Stanley D. Bachrack, *The Committee of One Million: "China Lobby" Politics, 1953–1971* (1976); Warren I. Cohen, *America's Response to China* (1971); Foster Rhea Dulles, *American Policy toward Communist China, 1949–1969* (1972); John King Fairbank, *The United States and China* (1979); Akira Iriye, *The Cold War in Asia* (1974); Michael Schaller, *The United States and China in the Twentieth Century* (1979); Robert G. Sutter, *China-Watch: Sino-American Reconciliation* (1978); and Kenneth T. Young, *Negotiating with the Chinese Communists: The United States Experience, 1953–1967* (1968).

Six books on American public opinion which give substantial attention to Cold War issues are Gabriel A. Almond, *The American People and Foreign Policy* (1950); Bernard C. Cohen, *The Public's Impact on Foreign Policy* (1973); Robert Dallek, *The American Style of Foreign Policy* (1983); Leonard A. Kusnitz, *Public Opinion and Foreign Policy; America's China Policy, 1949–1979* (1984); Ralph B. Levering, *The Public and American Foreign Policy, 1918–1978* (1978); and John E. Mueller, *War, Presidents and Public Opinion* (1973). James Aronson, *The Press and the Cold War* (1970), is an overly critical analysis of anti-communism in American newspapers and magazines. William Welch, *American Images of Soviet Foreign Policy* (1970), provides a more scholarly critique of American academic writing about the Soviet Union.

Chapter One (1945–1953)

The scholarly debate on the origins of the Cold War was most intense during the late 1960s. The orthodox viewpoint, which tended to blame Russia, is epitomized in Arthur Schlesinger, Jr., "Origins of the Cold War," *Foreign Affairs* 46 (October 1967): 22–52. The revisionist viewpoint, which tended to blame the United States, is ably expressed in Baron J. Bernstein, "American Foreign Policy and the Origins of the Cold War," in Bernstein, ed., *Politics and Policies of the Truman Administration* (1970), pp. 15–77. The best brief analysis of the early Cold War is Thomas G. Paterson, *On Every Front; The Making of the Cold War* (1979). Other excellent introductions to the period include a one-volume presidential biography by Donald R. McCoy: *The Presidency of Harry S. Truman* (1984); and a two-volume biography by Robert J. Donovan: *Conflict and Crisis* (1977) and *Tumultuous Years* (1983).

Partly because of the tendency to proceed from the assumption that either Russia or America was largely responsible for precipitating the Cold War, much of the writing on Cold War origins before 1970 was not as carefully researched and judiciously argued as the best writing was thereafter. An exception would be any of the many books on the 1940s by Herbert Feis which, while written from an American viewpoint, were based on thorough research in primary sources.

Drawing upon ample primary source materials, especially for American policy, numerous books and articles published between 1970 and 1981 established a new standard for judging scholarly writing on the Cold War. These include: Diane Shaver Clemens, *Yalta* (1970); Lynn Etheridge Davis, *The Cold War Begins: Soviet-American Conflict Over Eastern Europe* (1974); Hugh De Santis, *The Diplomacy of Silence* (1981); John Lewis Gaddis, *The United States and The Origins of the Cold War, 1941–1947* (1972); Lloyd C. Gardner, *Architects of Illusion* (1970); Alonzo L. Hamby, *Beyond the New Deal* (1973): Gregg F. Herken, *The Winning Weapon* (1981); George C. Herring, Jr., *Aid to Russia 1941–1946* (1973); Bruce Kuklick, *American Policy and the Division of Germany* (1972); Bruce R. Kuniholm, *The Origins of the Cold War in the Near East* (1980); Geir Lundestad, *The American Non-Policy Towards Eastern Europe, 1943–1947* (1975) and *America, Scandinavia, and the*

Cold War (1980); Robert J. McMahon, *Colonialism and Cold War* (1981); Vojtech Mastny, *Russia's Road to the Cold War, 1941–1945* (1979); Thomas G. Paterson, *Soviet-American Confrontation* (1973); Martin J. Sherwin, *A World Destroyed* (1975); Gaddis Smith, *Dean Acheson* (1972); William Stueck, *The Road to Confrontation* (1981); J. Samuel Walker, *Henry A. Wallace and American Foreign Policy* (1976); Patricia Dawson Ward, *The Threat of Peace* (1979); and Daniel Yergin, *Shattered Peace* (1978).

Important works on the early Cold War years published since 1981 include Paul Boyer, *By the Bomb's Early Light* (1985); Fraser J. Harbutt, *The Iron Curtain* (1986); Robert L. Messer, *The End of an Alliance* (1982); Norman A. Graebner, ed., *The National Security; Its Theory and Practice, 1945–1960* (1986); James Edward Miller, *The United States and Italy, 1940–1950* (1986); Robert A. Pollard, *Economic Security and the Origins of the Cold War* (1985); Avi Shlaim, *The United States and the Berlin Blockade, 1948–1949* (1983); and Lawrence Wittner, *American Intervention in Greece, 1943–1949* (1982).

It should be kept in mind that the scholarly studies I shall list for the years since 1950 generally have not been based on equally thorough research in official documents, simply because some records for the 1950s have become available only recently, and many records for the years since 1961 are still quite difficult to obtain. Some of the most important official records of the Truman years have been assembled in Thomas H. Etzold and John Lewis Gaddis, eds., *Containment: Documents on American Policy and Strategy, 1945–1950* (1978).

Students of American diplomacy between 1945 and 1953 have been aided by numerous published memoirs and diaries. The following are valuable examples: Dean Acheson, *Present at the Creation: My Years in the State Department* (1969); John Morton Blum, ed., *The Price of Vision: The Diary of Henry A. Wallace 1942–1946* (1973); Charles E. Bohlen, *Witness to History: 1929–1969* (1973); James F. Byrnes, *Speaking Frankly*

(1947); Lucius D. Clay, *Decision in Germany* (1950); Milovan Djilas, *Conversations with Stalin* (1962); W. Averell Harriman and Elie Abel, *Special Envoy to Churchill and Stalin, 1941–1946* (1975); Joseph M. Jones, *The Fifteen Weeks* (1965); George F. Kennan, *Memoirs*, 2 vols. (1967, 1972); Walter Millis, ed., *The Forrestal Diaries* (1951); Walter Bedell Smith, *My Three Years in Moscow* (1950); and Harry S. Truman, *Memoirs*, 2 vols. (1955, 1956).

For American policy toward China, in addition to the general works cited above, see John Robinson Beal, *Marshall in China* (1970); E. J. Kahn, *The China Hands: America's Foreign Service Officers and What Befell Them* (1976); Ross Y. Koen, *The China Lobby in American Politics* (1960); Gary May, *China Scapegoat: The Diplomatic Ordeal of John Carter Vincent* (1979); Ernest R. May, *The Truman Administration and China, 1945–1949* (1975); David Allan Meyers, *Cracking the Monolith; U.S. Policy Against the Sino-Soviet Alliance, 1949–1955* (1986); William Stueck, *The Wedemeyer Mission* (1984); Nancy Bernkopf Tucker, *Patterns in the Dust* (1982); Dorothy Borg and Waldo Heinrichs, eds., *The Uncertain Years: Chinese-American Relations, 1947–1950* (1981). On U.S. policy toward Japan, see Michael Schaller, *The American Occupation of Japan* (1985).

Finally, useful books on postwar Korea and the Korean War include Ronald J. Caridi, *The Korean War and American Politics* (1969); Bruce Cumings, *Child of Conflict* (1983); Rosemary Foot, *The Wrong War* (1985); F. H. Heller, ed., *The Korean War: A 25-Year Perspective* (1977); Burton I. Kaufman, *The Korean War* (1986); James Irving Matray, *The Reluctant Crusade* (1985); Glen Paige, *The Korean Decision: June 23–30, 1950* (1968); David Rees, *Korea: The Limited War* (1964); Robert R. Simmons, *The Strained Alliance* (1975); John W. Spanier, *The Truman-MacArthur Controversy and the Korean War* (1965); and Allen S. Whiting, *China Crosses the Yalu* (1960).

Chapter Two (1953–1962)

A good place to begin is Eisenhower's memoirs: *Mandate for Change, 1953–1956* (1963) and *Waging Peace, 1956–1961* (1965). Solid general accounts (largely favorable to Eisenhower) include Charles L. Alexander, *Holding the Line* (1975); Robert A. Divine, *Eisenhower and the Cold War* (1981); Townsend Hoopes, *The Devil and John Foster Dulles* (1973); Herbert S. Parmet, *Eisenhower and the American Crusades* (1972); and Elmo Richardson, *The Presidency of Dwight D. Eisenhower* (1979). The best study of Dulles's early career is Ronald Pruessen, *John Foster Dulles* (1982).

Russian foreign policy in the 1950s and early 1960s is described vividly in Nikita S. Khrushchev, *Khrushchev Remembers* (1970), and *Khrushchev Remembers: The Last Testament* (1974). Another useful Russian source for this period is Roy A. Medvedev, *On Stalin and Stalinism* (1979). In addition to the works by Ulam listed above, two valuable studies by American scholars are Thomas W. Wolfe, *Soviet Power and Europe: 1945–1970* (1970), and William Zimmerman, *Soviet Perspectives on International Relations, 1956–1967* (1967).

Books focusing on particular aspects of Soviet-American relations include Richard A. Aliano, *American Defense Policy from Eisenhower to Kennedy* (1975); Coral Bell, *Negotiating from Strength* (1963); Michael R. Beschloss, *Mayday; The U-2 Affair* (1986); Edgar M. Bottome, *The Missile Gap* (1971); Alexander L. George and Richard Smoke, *Deterrence in American Foreign Policy* (1974); and Jack M. Schick, *The Berlin Crisis, 1958–1962* (1971). American policy in the Middle East is analyzed in Wilbur Crane Eveland, *Ropes of Sand* (1980); and Donald Neff, *Warriors at Suez* (1981). A systematic study of the use of American military power abroad during the Cold War is Barry M. Blechman and Stephen S. Kaplan, *Force without War* (1978). On economic issues, see Burton I. Kaufman, *Trade and Aid: Eisenhower's Foreign Economic Policies, 1953–*

1961 (1982). Two fine recent studies of U.S. policy in the Caribbean area are Richard H. Immerman, *The CIA in Guatemala* (1982), and Richard E. Welch, Jr., *Response to Revolution; The United States and the Cuban Revolution, 1959–1961* (1985). For policy toward Africa, see Richard D. Mahoney, *JFK: Ordeal in Africa* (1983) and Thomas J. Noer, *Cold War and Black Liberation* (1985).

An early book on the threat of the Cold War to America's domestic institutions is Harold D. Lasswell, *National Security and Individual Freedom* (1950). Two representative works on the military-industrial complex are Fred J. Cook, *The Warfare State* (1962), and Carroll Pursell, Jr., ed., *The Military-Industrial Complex* (1972). A careful study of the movement against nuclear testing in the 1950s is Robert A. Divine, *Blowing on the Wind* (1978). The domestic underpinnings of the Cold War are decried in Richard J. Barnet, *Roots of War* (1972); Seymour Melman, *The Permanent War Economy* (1974); Michael Parenti, *The Anti-Communist Impulse* (1969); and Arthur M. Schlesinger, Jr., *The Imperial Presidency* (1973). The exposure of U.S. soldiers and civilians in nuclear testing is discussed in Howard L. Rosenberg, *Atomic Soldiers* (1980), and Howard Ball, *Justice Downwind* (1986).

In recent years, the literature on the foreign and domestic activities of American intelligence agencies during the 1950s and 1960s has become quite extensive. A good early study is David Wise and Thomas B. Ross, *The Invisible Government* (1964). Four recent works are Morton H. Halperin et al., *The Lawless State* (1976); John Prados, *Presidents' Secret Wars* (1986); John Ranelagh, *The Agency* (1987); and Thomas Powers, *The Man Who Kept the Secrets* (1979).

Many of the best-known books on the Kennedy years were written either by members of the administration or by journalists. Books by officials (often with academic backgrounds) include Roger Hilsman, *To Move a Nation* (1967); Robert Kennedy, *Thirteen Days* (1969); Arthur M. Schlesinger, Jr., *A Thousand Days* (1965); Glenn T. Seaborg, *Kennedy, Khrushchev, and the Test Ban* (1981); and Theodore Sorensen, *Ken-*

nedy (1965). Four stimulating books by journalists are Elie Abel, *The Missile Crisis* (1966); Henry Fairlie, *The Kennedy Promise* (1972); David Halberstam, *The Best and the Brightest* (1972); and Richard J. Walton, *Cold War and Counter-revolution* (1972).

Useful scholarly studies of this period include Graham T. Allison, *Essence of Decision: Explaining the Cuban Missile Crisis* (1971); Herbert S. Dinerstein, *The Making of a Missile Crisis* (1976); Montague Kern et al., *The Kennedy Crises* (1983); Bruce Miroff, *Pragmatic Illusions* (1976); Herbert S. Parmet, *JFK* (1981); Robert M. Slusser, *The Berlin Crisis of 1961* (1973); and Stephen Weissman, *American Foreign Policy in the Congo, 1960–1964* (1974). An interesting analysis of American attitudes toward Russia in 1961 is Stephen B. Withey, *The U.S. and the U.S.S.R.* (1962). For a Russian perspective on the early 1960s, see A. A. Gromyko, *Through Russian Eyes: President Kennedy's 1,036 Days* (1973).

Of the books on the Kennedy years cited above, those by officials, not surprisingly, are all highly favorable toward the administration's foreign policy. The ones by Fairlie, Halberstam, Walton, and Miroff are sharply critical on Vietnam and other issues. They represent a viewpoint that was especially strong at the height of the Vietnam War in the late 1960s and early 1970s.

Chapter Three (1963–1972)

The improvement in Soviet-American relations in 1963 is discussed in the Schlesinger and Sorensen books cited above, and in greater detail in Christer Jonsson, *Soviet Bargaining Behavior: The Nuclear Test Ban Case* (1979); and Ronald J. Terchek, *The Making of the Test Ban Treaty* (1970). Aspects of Soviet foreign policy in the 1960s and early 1970s are analyzed in Archie Brown and Michael Kaser, eds., *The Soviet Union Since the Fall of Khrushchev* (1975); Robin Edmonds, *Soviet Foreign Policy, 1962–1973* (1975); Michel Tatu, *Power in the*

Kremlin (1969); and Jiri Valenta, *Soviet Intervention in Czech-oslovakia, 1968* (1979). An early study of the Sino-Soviet split is Edward Crankshaw, *The New Cold War: Moscow v. Peking* (1963).

Partly because of the intense controversy over America's policy in Vietnam, much of the writing on the Johnson years is biased either against or (less often) in favor of the administration. For the administration's viewpoint, see Lyndon Baines Johnson, *The Vantage Point* (1971); and chapters 28–41 of W. W. Rostow, *The Diffusion of Power* (1972). A highly critical study is Theodore Draper, *The Abuse of Power* (1967). Four additional books that contain useful information are Warren Cohen, *Dean Rusk* (1980); Philip Geyelin, *Lyndon B. Johnson and the World* (1966); Abraham F. Lowenthal, *The Dominican Intervention* (1972); and Richard E. Neustadt, *Alliance Politics* (1970).

The literature on the Vietnam War is voluminous. The study that provides not only the most thorough documentation but also repeated examples of the Cold War mind-set is *The Pentagon Papers: The Senator Gravel Edition*, 5 vols. (1972). The best general secondary study is George C. Herring, Jr., *America's Longest War* (1979). Other works of unusual merit include Larry Berman, *Planning a Tragedy* (1982); Frances Fitzgerald, *Fire in the Lake* (1972); Townsend Hoopes, *The Limits of Intervention* (1969); Stanley Karnow, *Vietnam: A History* (1983); Gabriel Kolko, *Anatomy of a War* (1985); Guenter Lewy, *America in Vietnam* (1978); Robert Shaplen, *Time Out of Hand* (1969); and Ralph K. White, *Nobody Wanted War* (1968). American involvement in Laos is discussed in Charles A. Stevenson, *The End of Nowhere* (1973); and in Fred Branfman, *Voices from the Plain of Jars: Life under an Air War* (1972). A controversial book on the Nixon administration's policy is William Shawcross, *Sideshow: Kissinger, Nixon and the Destruction of Cambodia* (1978).

Perhaps the best overview of American policy toward China in the 1960s is James C. Thomson, Jr., "On the Making of U.S. China Policy, 1961-9: A Study in Bureaucratic Politics," *China Quarterly*, April–June 1972. A more detailed study is Kwan Ha Yim, ed., *China and the U.S. 1964–1972* (1975). For the Johnson years, see also Morton H. Halperin, *China and the Bomb* (1965); David Mozingo, *Chinese Foreign Policy and the Cultural Revolution* (1970); and A. T. Steele, *The American People and China* (1966). Nixon's policies receive attention in Jerome A. Cohen, ed., *Taiwan and American Foreign Policy* (1971); Lloyd C. Gardner, ed., *The Great Nixon Turnaround* (1973); and Earl C. Ravenal, ed., *Peace with China?* (1971).

Useful general accounts of the Nixon administration's approach to world affairs include Henry Brandon, *The Retreat of American Power* (1973); Robert E. Osgood et al., *Retreat From Empire?* (1973); and Tad Szulc, *The Illusion of Peace* (1978). The administration's thinking is outlined in Richard M. Nixon, *United States Foreign Policy for the 1970s* (1971); and Lester A. Sobel, ed., *Kissinger & Détente* (1975). A Russian viewpoint is Leonid Brezhnev, *On the Policy of the Soviet Union and the International Situation* (1973).

Two detailed defenses of administration policy are Richard Nixon, *RN: The Memoirs of Richard Nixon* (1978); and Henry Kissinger, *The White House Years* (1979). Another first-hand account is William Safire, *Before the Fall* (1975). Among the numerous studies of Kissinger's diplomacy, perhaps the most useful are Seyom Brown, *The Crises of Power* (1979); Seymour Hersh, *The Price of Power* (1983); Roger Morris, *Uncertain Greatness* (1977); and Harvey Starr, *Henry Kissinger; Perceptions of International Politics* (1984).

The most important book on the negotiation of the SALT I treaty is John Newhouse, *Cold Dawn* (1973). A useful collection of documents and essays on the SALT process is Mason Willrich and John B. Rhinelander, eds., *SALT: The Moscow Agreements and Beyond* (1974). Other useful books on military developments and the arms control process in the 1960s and 1970s include John M. Collins, *American and Soviet Military Trends Since the Cuban Missile Crisis* (1978); Ted Greenwood,

Making the MIRV (1975); Jerome H. Kahan, *Security in the Nuclear Age* (1975); and Herbert York, *Race to Oblivion* (1970).

Chapter Four (1973–1987)

Students of Soviet-American relations in the 1970s and early 1980s should turn first to Raymond L. Garthoff, *Detente and Confrontation; American-Soviet Relations from Nixon to Reagan* (1985). Other valuable books with broad coverage of the period since the early 1970s include Coit D. Blacker, *Reluctant Warriors: The United States, the Soviet Union, and Arms Control* (1987); Ole R. Holsti and James N. Rosenau, *American Leadership in World Affairs: Vietnam and the Breakdown of Consensus* (1984); Richard Smoke, *National Security and the Nuclear Dilemma* (1984); Alexander L. George, ed., *Managing U.S.-Soviet Rivalry: Problems of Crisis Prevention* (1983); David Holloway, *The Soviet Union and the Arms Race* (1983); William G. Hyland, *Mortal Rivals; Superpower Relations from Nixon to Reagan* (1987); Nish Jamgotch, Jr., *Sectors of Mutual Benefit in U.S.-Soviet Relations* (1985); Joseph S. Nye, Jr., ed., *The Making of America's Soviet Policy* (1984); Marshall D. Shulman, ed., *East-West Tensions in the Third World* (1986); Adam B. Ulam, *Dangerous Relations: The Soviet Union in World Politics, 1970–1982* (1983); and Sanford J. Ungar, ed., *Estrangement: America and the World* (1985). An interesting personal account of Soviet foreign policy, by an official who defected to the United States, is Arkady N. Shevchenko, *Breaking with Moscow* (1985).

For the years 1973–1976, see especially the Garthoff book listed above and the two works by Gaddis listed at the beginning of the bibliography. Other useful books include the second volume of Henry Kissinger's memoirs, *Years of Upheaval* (1983), and Gerald Ford's memoirs, *A Time to Heal* (1979). See also Arnold R. Isaacs, *Without Honor: Defeat in Vietnam and Cambodia* (1983); Robert C. Johansen, *The National Interest and the Human Interest* (1980); Thomas W. Wolfe, *The*

Salt Experience (1979); Thomas Franck and Edward Weisband, *Foreign Policy by Congress* (1979); Alan Platt, *The U.S. Senate and Strategic Arms Policy, 1969–1977* (1978); and Richard W. Stevenson, *The Rise and Fall of Detente* (1985). For a first-hand account of CIA activities in Angola, see John Stockwell, *In Search of Enemies* (1978).

The place to begin for the Carter years is Gaddis Smith, *Morality, Reason and Power: American Diplomacy in the Carter Years* (1986), which should be supplemented by the more detailed analysis of Soviet-American relations in the Garthoff book cited above. The memoirs of the three principals are instructive, especially when read together: Jimmy Carter, *Keeping Faith* (1982); Cyrus Vance, *Hard Choices* (1983); and Zbigniew Brzezinski, *Power and Principle* (1983). For arms control, see Strobe Talbott, *Endgame: The Inside Story of SALT II* (1979). For the Soviet-American rivalry in Africa, see Gerald J. Bender et al., *African Crisis Areas and U.S. Foreign Policy* (1985). For Afghanistan, see Henry S. Bradsher, *Afghanistan and the Soviet Union* (1985). The conservative critique of U.S. policy in the late 1970s is discussed in Jerry W. Sanders, *Peddlers of Crisis* (1983).

Strobe Talbott has written two excellent studies of Soviet-American relations in the early 1980s: *The Russians and Reagan* (1984), and *Deadly Gambits; The Reagan Administration and the Stalemate in Nuclear Arms Control* (1984). For relations since 1984, see Michael Mandelbaum and Strobe Talbott, *Reagan and Gorbachev* (1987). Other useful books on the early 1980s include Laurence I. Barrett, *Gambling with History* (1983); Robert Scheer, *With Enough Shovels* (1982); Alexander M. Haig, Jr., *Caveat* (1984); Alexander Dallin, *Black Box: KAL 007 and the Superpowers* (1985); Walter Goldstein, ed., *Reagan's Leadership and the Atlantic Alliance* (1986); and Douglas C. Waller, *Congress and the Nuclear Freeze* (1987).

The literature on Reagan's military buildup and on current issues in nuclear strategy and arms control is voluminous. Some of the more interesting works include Graham T. Allison et al., eds., *Hawks, Doves, and Owls: An Agenda for Avoiding*

Nuclear War (1985); Len Ackland and Steven McGuire, eds., *Assessing the Nuclear Age* (1986); Barry M. Blechman, ed., *Preventing Nuclear War* (1985); Paul Bracken, *The Command and Control of Nuclear Forces* (1983); William P. Bundy, ed., *The Nuclear Controversy* (1985); Paul M. Cole and William J. Taylor, Jr., *The Nuclear Freeze Debate* (1983); Norman Cousins, *The Pathology of Power* (1987); Tom Gervasi, *The Myth of Soviet Military Supremacy* (1986); Morton H. Halperin, *Nuclear Fallacy* (1987); George F. Kennan, *The Nuclear Delusion* (1983); Michael Krepon, *Strategic Stalemate* (1984); Robert S. McNamara, *Blundering into Disaster* (1986); Jonathan Schell, *The Fate of the Earth* (1982), and *The Abolition* (1984); Gene Sharp, *Making Europe Unconquerable* (1985); Paul B. Stares, *Space and National Security* (1987); John Tirman, ed., *The Fallacy of Star Wars* (1984); William L. Ury, *Beyond the Hotline* (1986); and Burns H. Weston, ed., *Toward Nuclear Disarmament and Global Security* (1984).

Reagan's policies in the Caribbean and Central America are discussed in Kenneth M. Coleman and George C. Herring, eds., *The Central America Crisis* (1985); Morris J. Blachman et al., *Confronting Revolution* (1986); James Chace, *Endless War* (1984); and Kai P. Schoenhals and Richard A. Melanson, *Revolution and Intervention in Grenada* (1985).

For changes in the Soviet Union and in Soviet foreign policy since Gorbachev's rise to power, see Martin Walker, *The Waking Giant; Gorbachev's Russia* (1986), and Mikhail S. Gorbachev, *Toward a Better World* (1987). The future of East-West relations also is discussed in Jonathan Dean, *Watershed in Europe* (1987); Arnold L. Horelick, ed., *U.S.-Soviet Relations; The Next Phase* (1986); and Edward Mortimer, *Roosevelt's Children* (1987).

INDEX

ABM treaty (1972), 124, 180, 182, 184
Acheson, Dean, 22, 29, 33–34, 36–37, 38, 40, 41, 43, 106
Adenauer, Konrad, 35, 65, 67
Afghanistan, 10, 155, 164–68, 170, 173, 179, 190, 196
AFL-CIO, 58, 62
Africa, 29, 141, 142–44, 158–61
  See also specific countries
Alsop, Joseph, 57
American Bar Association, 56
Americans for Democratic Action, 109
Anderson, John, 168
Andropov, Yuri, 172, 173
Angola, 142, 143–44, 166
Arab oil embargo (1973–1974), 141
Argentina, 167
Asia, 14, 15, 19–20, 23, 29, 37, 38, 41, 43, 66, 103, 109
  See also specific countries
Atomic Energy Commission, 61
atomic weapons and arms control, 20–23, 55, 61, 66, 67, 68–69, 78–79, 81, 83, 89, 96, 99–102, 110, 112–13, 115, 116, 124–25, 133, 135–36, 139, 144–46, 151–52, 155, 156, 157–58, 169–70, 171, 172, 173, 180–86, 189–91, 196
Attlee, Clement, 23
Australia, 65

Austria, 36
Aviation Week, 59

Bandung Conference (1955), 63
Baruch, Bernard, 22
Bay of Pigs (1961), 73, 86–87, 90, 93
Berlin, 14, 34–36, 37, 48, 55, 72, 77, 79–80, 81, 83, 87–89, 96, 105, 124
Bernstein, Barton J., 47
Blaufarb, Douglas S., 98
Bohlen, Charles, 2, 67
Boy Scouts, 57
Bradley, Omar, 47
Brandt, Willy, 124
Brezhnev, Leonid, 98, 126, 135–37, 139, 145, 158, 163, 165, 172
British Guiana, 62, 95
Brookings Institution, 72
Brown, Harold, 161
Brzezinski, Zbigniew, 71–72, 155–57, 160–62, 166, 167
Bukovsky, Vladimir, 157
Bulganin, Nikolai, 68
Bulgaria, 16
Bundy, McGeorge, 104
Burt, Richard, 171–72
Bush, George, 168
Byrnes, James, 16, 17, 18, 22, 28

Cambodia, 121, 127–28

Slepak, Vladimir, 157
Smith, Kingsbury, 36
Snow, Edgar, 129
Solzhenitsyn, Alexander, 26
Somalia, 59–61
Sorenson, Theodore, 93
South Africa, 143–44
Southeast Asia Treaty Organization
 (SEATO), 64, 65
South Korea
 See Korea, Korean airliner
 incident, Korean War
Souvanna Phouma, 84
Soviet Union, 29, 62
 Brezhnev's policy toward U.S.,
  111–13, 123–26, 135–37, 151,
  157–58
 and Cold War origins, 11–13, 15–
  27
 cultural exchanges with U.S., 70–
  71, 113, 136, 167, 191
 defense policy, 21–22, 39, 78–79,
  112–13
 domestic effects of the Cold War,
  55–56
 effects of World War II on, 14–15
 Gorbachev's policy toward U.S.,
  180–85
 intervention in Afghanistan, 164–
  68
 Khrushchev's policy toward U.S.,
  53–54, 64, 66–96
 myths, 7–9
 policy at Yalta Conference, 3–7
 policy toward Korea, 43–48
 policy toward U.S. in late 1970s
  and early 1980s, 157–74
 policy toward Vietnam, 106, 111–
  12, 115, 120, 123
 response to containment policy,
  33–36
Spain, 38
Sputnik I, 78–79, 81
Stalin, Josef, 3–6, 11–12, 15, 16–17,
 18, 19, 20, 21–22, 24, 25–26, 32–
 37, 43, 44–45, 49, 50, 51, 53, 63,
 66, 67, 73, 79, 95, 192
State Department, U.S., 27, 29, 31,
 42–43, 60, 67, 77, 125, 139, 149,
 156–57, 160, 167, 176

Stevenson, Adlai, 77
Stoessinger, John G., 117
Strategic Defense Initiative ("Star
 Wars"), 180–84
Strauss, Lewis L., 61
Students for a Democratic Society
 (SDS), 109, 121
Suez crisis (1956), 74–77, 96
Survey Research Center polls, 35
Symington, Stuart, 78
Syria, 62, 113, 114, 136

Taft, Robert, 25, 42
Taiwan:
 See China, Republic of
test ban treaty (1963), 99–102
Thailand, 105
Thatcher, Margaret, 175, 182
Time, 5, 36, 37, 57
Tito, Josip Broz, 32–33, 74, 102
Truman Doctrine (1947), 29–30, 34,
 36
Truman, Harry S., 8, 11–12, 15, 16,
 17, 20, 21, 23, 25, 26–27, 28, 29–
 30, 32, 33, 34, 36, 39, 41, 43, 45,
 48–49, 50, 64, 85, 95, 104, 106
Truman Margaret, 27
Turkey, 15, 17–18, 29, 30, 36, 42,
 58, 91

U-2 incident (1960), 81–82
Ulam, Adam B., 33, 64
Ulbricht, Walter, 79, 88
United Nations, 2, 3, 22, 36, 43, 44,
 45, 54, 91, 95, 110, 114, 130, 136,
 193
United States:
 Carter's policy toward China,
  154, 161–63
 Carter's policy toward Russia,
  155–68
 Cold War myths, 7–9
 and Cold War origins, 11–13, 15–
  29
 containment policy, 29–37
 covert operations abroad, 33, 37,
  50, 61–63, 65, 73, 81–82, 84,
  86–87, 108, 122, 136, 141
 defense policy, 32, 35, 38, 39, 55,
  59–60, 65–66, 77–79, 80, 87–88

The Cold War, 1945–1987, Second Edition was copyedited and proofread by Martha Kreger. Production editor was Brad Barrett. Two new maps were prepared by James A. Bier. New material was typeset by Impressions, Inc., and the book was printed and bound by Lithocolor Press.

The cover illustration is by Hermann Degkwitz.